Gardens of France

Gardens of France

Anita Pereire   Gabrielle van Zuylen

Photographs by Robert César

Harmony Books / New York

The illustration on the
half-title page shows
rhododendrons in the Parc
Floral des Moutiers, near
Dieppe.

The title pages show
massed irises at Jas Créma,
Haute Provence.

First published in Great Britain in 1983 by
George Weidenfeld and Nicolson Ltd
91 Clapham High Street, London, SW4 7TA

Published in the United States in 1983 by Harmony Books, a division of Crown Publishers, Inc.,
One Park Avenue, New York, New York 10016 HARMONY and Colophon are trademarks of Crown Publishers, Inc.

Library of Congress Cataloging in Publication Data

Pereire, Anita.
    Gardens of France.

    1. Gardens—France.   I. Van Zuylen, Gabrielle.
II. Title.
SB466.F8P46   1983   914.4′04838   83–10726
ISBN 0–517–55125–X

Designed by Simon Bell, assisted by Patrick Frean and
Gillian Riley

Filmset by Keyspools Ltd, Golborne, Lancashire
Color separations by Newsele Litho Ltd.
Printed in Italy
First Edition   10 9 8 7 6 5 4 3 2 1

Contents

Foreword

by Marghanita Laski

ANITA PEREIRE is the oldest good friend that I have. We met as schoolgirls in Paris and consorted together in Hampstead as we grew up. Anyone who met us then might, I think now, have guessed that we would both grow up to be journalists. What no one – not even Anita and I – could have supposed is that two such quintessentially urban young girls would come, each in her own way, to a passion for gardens.

Mine is the lazy passion, that of the on-looker, sightseer, and reader. Anita Pereire has these devotions too, but she is (as I have always known her to be) far more energetically pro-fessional than I am; and when I bought a house in France some fifteen years ago and began to make something of a garden there, I was very conscious of my good fortune in finding her syndicated gardening column in even our very local newspaper. If anything is to teach the new French gardeners in the new suburban villas how to make really good gardens, it will be such excellent gardening programmes and columns as Anita Pereire presents in France.

But behind the small arts of the little domestic garden must always lie a country's great gardens, and, as this book can show us, the French no more lack fine models than we do. Indeed, the French have had, since the introduction of the *jardin anglais* some 200 years ago, a flattering liking for our English gardens. But if we took our inspiration from such few formal gardens as we went in for rather from Holland than from France, the *idea* of the later French gardens has for us an enormous roman-tic force. Those of us who are both Fran-cophiles and novel-readers know on the pulse (as John Keats put it) that we will find happiness in those essentially French gardens,

no matter how small and no matter how neglected – whether in the clear light of Normandy that ravished our poets and painters a century ago, or in the secluded elegance of hidden beauty in the Ile de France, or (for us the supreme dream) in the south, in that Provence that eighteenth-century English travellers like Arthur Young contrived to find such a depressing landscape: all those dark ilexes, all those monotonously silver olive trees. Yet not least among the dreams that we English find realized in this book will be those of the gardens of the 'sweet south'.

For me, however, one garden in this book is special, not only for beauty but for friendship too. This is Anita Pereire's own garden at the Abbaye de l'Eau near Chartres. Having been able, then, not only to read the manuscript of this book but even to wander in one of its gardens, it is both a privilege and a delight to be able to introduce the book of these two authors to their garden-loving public.

Foreword

by Russell Page O.B.E., F.I.L.A

EACH COUNTRY has its own gardening characteristics, and the rules which have shaped
French gardens differ from those that define
the gardens of Britain and Italy. In comparison
with British and Italian gardens, the picturesque element in French gardens is a late
arrival. Orderliness was always their main
feature: as a source of raw materials for the
pleasures of the table, the French kitchen
garden has always been laid out as impeccably
as the wine bottles in the cellar and the linen in
the closet. Pleasure gardens developed as a
decorative extension of the house they surrounded, whether in the formal manner which
survived until the second half of the eighteenth century, or in the winding convolutions
of paths, lawns, shrubberies and flower-beds
that were popular from 1820 to 1920.

It was not until after the Second World War
that the informal English style of garden
became generally known and appreciated in
France. The economic burden of château life
did not suit the younger generation's tastes or
pockets: they wanted swimming pools, tennis
courts and gardens that could be managed by
one man, and they came to enjoy gardening for
its own sake. Herbaceous borders became
fashionable, as they were both labour-saving
and colourful, and a wider range of flowering
shrubs replaced aucubas, Portuguese laurel and
Viburnum rhytidophyllum. Finally lawns, which
formerly had simply been fields mown to set off
perspectives of lakes and hills and clumps of
trees, found a new popularity.

Gardening and horticulture have made great
strides in France since the war. Now there is an
ever-increasing range of flowering plants and
more and more knowledgeable amateur gardeners. The late Vicomte Charles de Noailles,
Roger and André de Vilmorin, the Princess de
Caraman Chimay, M. Jacques Prévosteau, M.
Tom Kernan, M. Marnier l'Apostole, M.
Arpad Plesch, Prince Wolkonsky, the Princess
Sturdza and Mogens Tvede are only some of
those who have set the highest standards in
gardening and generously shared not only their
knowledge and enthusiasm, but also their
plants and cuttings.

Gabrielle van Zuylen is herself an accomplished and practical gardener, as her gardens
in Normandy and Holland testify. With her
you will enjoy visiting the gardens of France,
old and new.

CALAIS

LILLE

0 40 80 120 160 km
0 20 40 60 80 100 miles

20
CHERBOURG

DIEPPE
17 *15*
16

AMIENS

LE HAVRE
12 *10* *11*
BAYEUX *13*
19 *14*

ROUEN

18

REIMS

STRASBOURG

BREST

ST BRIEUC

21

RENNES

25

LE MANS

26

ORLEANS

DIJON

NANTES

TOURS
27

NEVERS
22

POITIERS *23*

LA ROCHELLE

LIMOGES

CLERMONT-
FERRAND

LYON

24
PERIGUEUX

BORDEAUX

28
CARPENTRAS

32 *29* *31*
CANNES *30*

BIARRITZ

TOULOUSE

MONTPELLIER

MARSEILLE

*Paris area –
see inset panel*

PERPIGNAN

Paris area

9

HOUDAN

PARIS

4

6 *8*

RAMBOUILLET

1

MELUN

CHARTRES *5*

2

7

0 20 40 km
0 10 20 miles

FONTAINEBLEAU

3

N

Introduction

THE HISTORY of the French garden is a history of loss. Marly, Maupertuis, Guiscard, Luzancy, Bellevue, the magic names crowd the mind – but all are gone, leaving only a few precious reminders of what the great age of garden design in France could achieve. Our aim in this book has been to record some of the fine gardens of France at a time of rebirth in French horticulture, with a revival of interest in the theory and practice of gardening. We have sought to keep a balance between the French classical garden and those gardens whose inspiration derives from the work of English gardeners of the last two centuries. We have dealt (with the sole exception of Monet's garden at Giverny) only with the gardens of privately owned and occupied houses – gardens which form part of a living domestic setting. Some are open to new influences, to growth and change; others are mysteriously timeless, rooted in the past and seemingly unchanging. But all spring from the history of the French garden.

Renaissance Italy derived its gardens from Rome, and the French in turn, having invaded Italy frequently in the sixteenth and seventeenth centuries, created their gardens from what they had learned from Palladio and Buontalenti. French gardens hitherto had been little more than tentative extensions of the modest plantings to be found in medieval monasteries; the first garden to be planned in conjunction with a dwelling is likely to have been at the Château of Anet (pp 64–9), designed by Philibert Delorme from 1547–56, but even this was still essentially medieval in feeling. At Dampierre the medieval moat at last ceased to impose a physical limit on the domestic area, and became adapted to an ornamental role. Then came Fouquet's Vaux-le-Vicomte (pp. 14–23), one of the first of the great French gardens, created by Le Nôtre, whose work at Versailles, which was to dominate the theory and practice of landscaping in France, was completed soon afterwards.

What France had imported from Italy was essentially the taste and the need for grandeur. The Italians achieved it largely from the steep terracing of their natural hillsides, but in France, with its flatter topography, another solution imposed itself: the creation of large vistas, innumerable fountains, parterres, boscages and arabesques of box hedging, and carefully drilled mosaics of flowerbeds – gardens to be admired from the luxury of a salon or the comfort of a carriage. Lucien Corpechot, writing about the gardens of the seventeenth and eighteenth centuries, entitled his work *Gardens of the Intelligence*. He understood very well the philosophy which lay behind Le Nôtre's royal walks and carefully aligned *pièces d'eau*: 'Icy, impersonal perfection . . . the beauty of a scene which unfolds entirely within the serene realm of logic.' These great gardens had nothing to do with the senses and everything to do with the mind.

Of the gardens explored in the present volume, Vaux-le-Vicomte best illustrates (though it is much modified) this spirit of seventeenth- and eighteenth-century rationalism. Versailles itself spread its influence across the face of Europe, and even back into Italy. Le Nôtre received a royal invitation to England, but in his independent way turned it down and sent his nephew instead. What effect might the old man's great prestige and powerful personality have had on the development of the

English garden had he crossed the Channel!

As it was, the English garden, dismissed as unruly, uncivilized and impossibly emotional, began to exert its magic in France as the *Ancien Régime* drew to its close and new ideas swept across Europe. The most eloquent champion of English methods was that extraordinary Marshal of France, the Prince de Ligne. The Prince, who built himself an English garden at Belœil on his way east to fight the Turks, had clear views, elegantly expressed. His great classic of gardening literature, *Coup d'Œil sur Belœil*, is a brilliantly sustained argument against the excessive taming of nature. '*Ne luttons jamais contre la nature, ni contre les saisons*': we should never struggle against nature, nor against the seasons. It was the antithesis of Versailles. His opinions were eclectic and civilized:

> More good sense in England, less order in France, less architecture in Italy, more wit in Holland, more sun in Russia, more trees in Hungary, more lawns in Germany, more richness in Switzerland, more taste everywhere, that is what I wish the gardeners of these countries. Apart from that, poetry, philosophy, sacrifices to nature. It is nature herself who should be the altar and the offering.

The spirit which informs *Coup d'Œil sur Belœil* was to make spectacular progress in France throughout the nineteenth century, and perhaps even more in the twentieth. There was no longer a need for endless walks down which kings and their guests could be drawn in picturesque carriages; and statuary designed to reassure a court that it existed by divine right was called for no longer once courts had shrunk or disappeared and the concept of divine right had lost its sway. And for those reasons many of the gardens illustrated here show the powerful influence of the great English gardeners. Stourhead and Sissinghurst are felt as strongly in these pages as Villandry, Vaux and Courances. Intelligence or sensibility? The geometry of Le Nôtre, Mollet and Gabriel or the carefully random effects of Capability Brown, Humphrey Repton and Gertrude Jekyll? There is room for both, and the great French gardens of today are often a synthesis of these diametrically opposed systems, further enriched by the exotic plantings made possible by the extraordinary variations in climate between the north and south of the country.

If one dared to anticipate the nature of the French garden of tomorrow, a clue might be found in our decision to include in this book Monet's garden at Giverny, although it is not really a privately owned garden any more. Here you find lush profusion, organized anarchy, riotous colour and a celebration of simple cottage plants, but all displayed within a symmetrical framework. A possible signpost to the future of garden design in France, it is a truly Impressionist garden, illustrating the words of Claudel: '*L'ordre est le plaisir de la raison, mais le désordre est le délire de l'imagination*': order is the pleasure of reason, but disorder is the frenzy of the imagination.

The authors are more than grateful to the owners and gardeners of the properties illustrated in these pages for their unfailing help, courtesy and knowledgeable advice, without which this book would have been impossible.

Vaux-le-Vicomte

near Melun
(Le Comte Patrice de Vogüé)

VAUX-LE-VICOMTE is the first great formal garden, laid out symmetrically in the grand manner. The seventeenth century, *le Grand Siècle*, found its symbol in the person of Louis XIV and its chief glory in Versailles – inspired largely by Nicolas Fouquet's creation of Vaux-le-Vicomte.

In 1641, Fouquet bought the *seigneurie* of Vaux-le-Vicomte: a small fortified castle and a scattering of houses, which was to grow into an estate of 6,000 hectares. In later years, Fouquet wrote from prison that it had been a place he thought of as his principal residence and where he wanted to leave the mark of his former high estate. To achieve his design he chose the collaboration of three remarkable men: the architect Louis Le Vau to design the plans of the château; Charles Le Brun to create the interiors, paint the ceilings, supervise the tapestries and even design the furniture and garden statuary; and lastly André Le Nôtre to plan the gardens and redesign the landscape. By 1650 he had spent over £16 million on the project: three villages near Melun had been bought, only to be razed, and 18,000 workers hired.

The twenty-two-year-old King took his first steps towards asserting his power and authority on the evening of 17 August, 1666. Fouquet, his 'Surintendant des Finances de France', had prepared an entertainment in the King's honour at his new château, Vaux-le-Vicomte. At three in the afternoon on that hot, sultry day the King left Fontainebleau, accompanied by Monsieur, his brother, the Duchesse de Valentinois, the Queen Mother, le Grand Condé, the Duc de Beaufort, the Duc de Guise, the Duc d'Enghien and other nobles. At Vaux preparations were feverish; the last scaffolding came down only as the King approached with

Two vast box embroidered parterres line the central axis of Le Nôtre's extraordinary garden.

The fountains of Vaux-le-Vicomte.

La Gerbe with a copy of
the Farnesian Hercules
cast in gilded lead.

La Couronne

Le Bassin de Triton.

Frogs add a rare touch of frivolity.

The Canal de la Pöele.

his retinue, and furniture and plate had been brought from Fouquet's houses in Paris, for this was to be an unforgettable *fête*. We will never know if this was ignorance or bravado in the face of the King's growing jealousy and the cold efficient enmity of his chief minister, Colbert.

At six o'clock the royal cortege passed the stone giants that still support the ironwork in front of the main courtyard. After visiting the château and its glories the King and Court went into the gardens to refresh themselves from the sullen heat of the day. La Fontaine wrote that there was much discussion as to which of the various marvels was the most beautiful: the walls of water springing up in unequal jets on either side of the central promenade, the cascades, or the various fountains. The King and his ladies took small carriages to the Canal de la Pöele, then climbed the hill of the Farnesian Hercules to view the extraordinary garden that stretched below them. Amazed by the quantity of water – for Versailles lacked even a pond – and deeply impressed by the gardens, the King toured the whole estate asking the names of those responsible. He sincerely congratulated Le Nôtre; the audacious extravagance of the undertaking was discreetly ignored, although blatantly visible to all.

Supper was served on plates of silver-gilt under Le Brun's magnificent painting of 'Le Palais du Soleil' the Sun Palace. Lully supplied background music with an ensemble of hidden string players. Later, Louis XIV and his courtiers returned to the triple terrace, the 'Grille d'Eau', where Molière and his troop acted his *Les Fâcheux de Vaux*, written for the occasion. Molière's wife, La Béjart, emerged Venus-like from a huge shell, to declaim a poem in honour of the King: '*Jeune, victorieux, sage, vaillant, auguste*'. After a second light supper of delicacies the King gave the signal for departure. As a final homage to his sovereign, Fouquet organized a display of fireworks behind the dome of the château, frightening the Queen Mother's horses into the moat. 'I do not think that such a fête should have so tragic and pitiful an ending' wrote La Fontaine prophetically to an absent friend.

The true ending of *la fête de Vaux* came two

The banks of La Pöele looking towards Les Grottes.

weeks later, when Fouquet was arrested by d'Artagnan. Fouquet, the patron and friend of La Fontaine, of Molière, of Le Brun and Le Nôtre, died nineteen years later in prison, and Vaux would never again know such an evening. The garden statues were plundered to embellish Le Nôtre's designs for Versailles, and even the orange trees were uprooted and transported by the over-impressed King.

If the fête at Vaux marked the end of Nicolas Fouquet's career, it was the beginning of André Le Nôtre's enormous influence. Both Le Nôtre's ancestry and his training were useful to him, but it was his personal genius that made him the greatest of European horticulturalists, 'the king of gardeners'. He came from a gardening family; his father, Jean, was head gardener at the Tuileries, his godmother was the wife of Claude Mollet, the great gardener who popularized the use of box hedges in embroidered parterres. As a young man, Le Nôtre studied painting in the studio of Simon Vouet (along with Le Brun, who became a lifelong friend) and throughout his long life his training in the visual arts was a means to sharpen and direct his eye. From painting he turned to architecture, probably working under Mansart, a discipline which must have corresponded to his inner sense of space and balance. In 1637 he succeeded his father, and in 1645 he redesigned the gardens of the Tuileries, imposing order and balance on the haphazard muddle laid out in front of the Louvre. The main plan, including the avenue of trees climbing the opposite hill, now the Champs-Elysées, remains very much the same today – simplification on a grand scale.

In 1661 André Le Nôtre completed his work at Vaux, opening up enormous perspectives through the gentle hills of the Ile de France. Sensitive to the possibilities of the landscape, he overcame the difficulties of a sloping site by raising a terrace and planting trees. Nature was subjected to the strict discipline of rectilinear lines, the château becoming the focal point from which they radiated.

The distribution of the terraces, large parterres, bosquets, and avenues of hornbeams was governed by slight indentations and minor declivities. Water played an essential role; high jets and flat mirrors to reflect the sky and give light to the garden. The vast parterres are bisected by the first broad canal which, like the larger main canal hidden behind the high stone colonnades of the *Petite Cascade*, is invisible from the terrace. The baroque stone statues and ornamental vases gave height to the plan and softened its severity slightly. Today, clipped yews have replaced the vanished statuary, and Le Nôtre's deliberate contrasting of white with dark tones of green has, alas, been lost.

Le Nôtre left no written record of the principles that he used on such a grand scale in his garden designs, and which ever since have inspired and shaped parks and gardens throughout the world. Le Blond's treatise, *The Theory and Practice of Gardening*, is the closest we can get to the rules underlying the composition of Vaux and Versailles. The four fundamentals laid down are, firstly, that art must give place to

ABOVE Tiber, the river god, sculpted by Lespagnandel, in the shelter of Les Grottes.
LEFT A lion at the base of a side retaining wall.

The majesty of Louis le Vau's château set in the perfect symmetry of Andre Le Nôtre's magnificent first gardens.

nature – that is, nature should be controlled but not perverted, trees should be left on hills, water on low ground. Secondly, large open spaces should be left around buildings to reveal the full perspective; thirdly, the garden should not be too open, and each view should have a stop. Lastly, a garden should always be made to look bigger than it is by having perspectives opened out over the surrounding countryside. For the attainment of the seventeenth-century ideal of magnificence more rigid rules were laid down: the obligatory large space next to the house should be equal in width to the height of the building from ground level to the cornice; walks should end in perspectives, with water replacing walls in the garden; the length of the garden should be one and a half times its breadth; and the main avenue or walk should run the length of the garden, starting from directly in front of the house. Although Le Nôtre did not set down these rules for the future, he nevertheless left us Vaux-le-Vicomte and Versailles as illustrations of his art.

Vaux is a Cartesian triumph, aesthetically and architecturally perfect, with well-proportioned spaces, long, serene vistas, and a

backdrop of trees chosen more for their uni-
formity of growth than for their beauty.
However, it never touches the heart, and
intellectual satisfaction is limited by a lack of
sensual pleasure. The gardens of Vaux should
be seen as a stage setting for the personalities of
le Grand Siècle, the intricate parterres designed
for the mannered movements of courtiers and
the glory of the master, and laid out like a vast
carpet to be admired from the sheltered secur-
ity of elaborate salons.

Over the next two centuries Vaux changed
hands several times, sliding slowly into decay,

and the gardens below the terraces became a
wheatfield. In 1875, Alfred Sommier, a wealthy
sugar merchant, bought the property from the
Choiseul-Praslins. His great-nephew Jean de
Vogüé, and his son in turn, have had Vaux
classified as a historic monument and opened
to the public. Historically, it is both logical and
satisfying that newly-acquired wealth should
have created this great domain, now restored
and saved by the Vogüés. Houses and
gardens, like works of art, appear to have
a destiny of their own; their own means of
survival.

Le Potager

Fleury-en-Bière

(La Duchesse de Mouchy)

THE DUCHESSE DE MOUCHY's jewel of a garden lies behind Virginia-creepered stone walls, beside the fine Romanesque church in the quiet village of Fleury. It is a garden to dream in and learn from, a cornucopia of ideas for the small garden.

Le Potager was virtually bare when the Duchesse de Mouchy came to Fleury in 1950, but she kept its few handsome trees to give bone structure to the future garden. Her cousin, the Danish architect Mogens Tvede, was to help with the layout of the three acres available.

Coming into the garden from the village street the first thing you see is a pretty arbour of spineless false acacias, *Robinia pseudoacacia bessoniana*, trained to form trellised arcades, with feathery branches breaking out halfway up each trunk and forming little green bouquets. A charming village custom has developed over the years: brides believe that it is lucky to be photographed under the pergola on their wedding day. Now many a family album opens with this first portrait of marital bliss

To the right of the pergola, against the high inner wall, lies a colourful border of delphiniums, day lilies and acanthus. Apart from some dahlias there are no annuals at Le Potager: a balance of shrubs and perennials makes the upkeep of the garden much easier and also gives a note of architectural elegance to the planting. On a small lawn to the left of the pergola stands an extraordinary topiary

The topiary sentry box of clipped thuya stands on a base of cobblestones.

A decorative urn under a weeping willow.

A blunt yew pyramid in the centre of the garden.

sentry box, complete with door, windows and a domed roof, made out of *Thuya lobii atrovirens*.

The Duchesse de Mouchy's house is neither over-elegant nor completely rustic. The old stone walls are covered with climbers: trellised pyracantha, the shade-loving *Hydrangea petiolaris*, and Virginia creeper mingling with two rose varieties – 'Aloa', pink shading into terracotta, and the disease-free 'New Dawn'. In front of the house, box topiary has been clipped to the elegant shapes of fleur-de-lis.

At the end of the house is a paved patio, where the family can sit in the sun. Two interesting trees are planted here: the mimosa-like *Albizia julibrissin*, a parasol of pink flowers in summer, and a *Cornus controversa*, with sweeping horizontal branches and striking silver variegated leaves. Aromatic and scented plants grow in large terracotta pots: lilies, citronella, heavily scented daturas and *Pelargonium tomentosum*. When the albizia make a pink canopy in summer one is transported to a sunny corner of the south of France.

A small path leads from the patio to the first of the garden 'rooms' – the herb garden, with squares of saxifrage, sedum, arum, lavender and old-fashioned pinks. The topiary parasols of *Cotoneaster sinensii*, trained on trellises to

ABOVE the mimosa-like *Albizia julibrissin* gives the patio a Mediterranean air in summer.

RIGHT The grass-bordered water at the end of the garden.

ABOVE Yews and clerodendron enclose the shady garden of St Antoine.

RIGHT The *trompe l'œil* satyr reflected in the pool at the bottom of the garden.

grow out of pyramids of clipped yew, give an architectural effect, and their red berries provide winter colour. Two sides of the herb garden are enclosed by yew hedges curving around large terracotta pots of fuchsias and pelargoniums. The wall between Le Potager and the village church makes another tiny garden, St Antoine's Garden, built around a statue of the saint. This is a calm, shady corner surrounded by yews and clerodendrons.

A pyramid-shaped tulip tree, *Liriodendron tulipifera fastifiatum*, stands like a column before the Persian Garden, so called because of the porphyry and marble mosaic floor in tones of grey, inspired by an old Persian geometric design. *Magnolia grandiflora* and the climbing *Hydrangea petiolaris* cover the walls.

The next garden, slightly lower, is enclosed by a hedge of clipped cotoneaster intermingled with roses and clematis. Here a *Parrotia persica's* gold and crimson autumn foliage shadows the silver *Stachys lanata*, set on broad swathes of lawn. Dark pyramid-shaped yews stand like statues in this silver and green garden.

The path winds gently towards the axis of the garden, a long central avenue. Four paths branch out from a central sundial, surrounded by yew and senecio 'White Diamond'. Yew squares filled with pink dahlias – a lovely variety named 'Marie Rose', unfortunately no longer obtainable – line one side of the walk.

Beyond stretches a lawn punctuated by a single tree: the outstandingly lovely golden-leaved *Robinia pseudoacacia frisia*. A group of silver poplars marks the boundary of the property, and beyond the cutting garden a pavilion is enclosed by a patchwork hedge, a mixture of holly, berberis, cotoneaster and pyracantha. The cutting garden is planted with an unusual array of lilies, arums, eucomis and spidery cleomes. At a slightly lower level a pool lies near the large trees of the neighbouring château, its only focal point a *Hydrangea aspera*. On the far side of the pool a satyr seems to be hiding in the undergrowth: this startling illusion is created by a flat cut-out *trompe-l'œil*, brought out and put in place in season. 'Madame la Duchesse's satyr is in the garden', proclaims the gardener, heralding the fine weather to come.

Château de Courances

near Fontainebleau
(Le Marquis et la Marquise de Ganay)

COURANCES is a masterpiece of harmony, equilibrium and clear, still waters. The visitor's first sight is of long rectangular pools forming flat mirrors on either side of the central aisle, a majestic avenue of century-old plane trees leading to the château. The dignity of the approach is magnified by the calm of the waters and the even splendour of the trees, lit by the '*jeux de miroirs*'.

The history of Courances can be traced back to the twelfth century, when it was owned by Guillaume de Milly. The *seigneurie* of Courances was to change hands often. In 1552 it was sold to Cosme Clausse, Henri II's banker. In 1682 the estate was sold again, this time to Claude Gallard, who brought in Gilles Le Breton to build the château. His son, also named Claude, is said to have had the garden designed and laid out by Le Nôtre. Beaubrun's portrait of his wife, Anne Vialart, 'La Dame de Gallard', painted in 1660, shows a bird's-eye view of the château and gardens after her father-in-law's transformation. An eighteenth-century plan gives further evidence of the

The serene *parterres à la française* and mirror basin set in a green landscape.

PREVIOUS PAGES
LEFT one of 'Les Gueulards', probably carved by the Italian artists brought to France to work on the Château of Fontainebleau.

PREVIOUS PAGES
RIGHT The Japanese garden on the island of *La Foulerie*.

ABOVE Lions and Roman wolves guard *Les Cascatelles*.

ABOVE RIGHT The sculpture called *La Baigneuse* came originally from the Château of Marly.

RIGHT Oak, beech, ash, lime and chestnut trees form the background for the canal of the Dolphin.

estate's historical evolution. Courances remained in the possession of the Gallards until the Revolution, when Aimard-Charles-Marie de Nicolay, called the Great Nicolay, and his eldest son were guillotined. Courances fell into decay, lost without trace beneath the rampant vegetation which took over the property as the years passed.

In 1872 the Baron de Haber, the present owner's great grandfather, bought Courances and began its restoration. The architect Destailleurs was brought in to restore the house and Achille Duchêne, a well-known garden architect of the period, was commissioned to restore the park to its former beauty: the basins were uncovered, the embroidered parterres replanted, and the eight radii forming the garden's basic skeleton redefined. Courances was once more reflected in its many mirrors. 'The whiteness and the currents in the waters of this place of beauty have given it the name of Courances': a fair description by Dezellier d'Argenville, as the park is full of natural springs of great purity. Water fills the canals and moat, flows down the cascades, falls back into the large peaceful basins, and pours from the mouths of stone dolphins. Referring to the '*grande salle d'eau*', Dezellier writes that in 1755 it was 'surrounded by fourteen dolphins, each throwing forth as much water as a mill wheel would need to turn'.

Courances is also famous for its stonework, all of it wonderfully mellowed by a mossy patina – stone wreaths forming balustrades, dolphins and playful *putti*, statues guarding the lateral avenues, nymphs and crouching lions. Although there is no actual proof of Le Nôtre's authorship of Courances, the magnificent equilibrium that his style imposed on whatever he touched is everywhere in evidence.

We tend to think of historical domains as static and fossilized, which is far from the truth. After the Liberation, in 1944, the Ganay family found Courances a scene of desolation. First occupied by the Germans, then converted into a prisoner-of-war camp by the Americans, the park was disfigured by a motley collection of buildings – workshops, garages, a cinema, endless offices and even a barber's shop. Water reeds had invaded the basins and truck tracks criss-crossed the park. Lawns and parterres had

been destroyed. At this sad period Courances was fortunate to have as its new owners the Marquis de Ganay, his son Jean-Louis, a graduate of the Agricultural College at Grignon, and his wife Philippine, now the acting President of the French Garden Society, *La Société des Amateurs des Jardins*. Courances became their home. Using equipment from the farm, and with the help of everyone working on the estate, the family set to work: buildings were dynamited, the *pièces d'eau* cleared, the lawns re-seeded, trees planted and, in direct contrast to French tradition, the avenues, formerly sanded, were replanted with grass. The Marquise de Ganay encouraged roses – the exuberant 'Kiftsgate' and the beautiful 'Rosemary Muir' – to climb over the balustrades. The bare stretches in front of the terraces at the foot of the château were transformed by careful planting. Magnolias were trained to cover walls, and *Choisya ternata* (the Mexican orange), santolinas, variegated ivies, *Daphne mezereum*, *Chimonanthus fragrans* and nepeta were introduced.

The following description of the gardens in front of the château comes from an erudite article written by the present owner, Hubert, Marquis de Ganay, and published in the *Gazette des Amateurs des Jardins*:

In front of the château, on the side where the moat borders the gardens, lies a large embroidered parterre, where well-placed shrubs provide congenial relief. The first of the ornamental basins lies beyond this decorative *terre-plein* along the unchanged axis of the median perspective, although the basin itself has changed in shape. The original circular basin disappeared during the eighteenth century and was replaced at the time by the present carved mirror basin. There another change has also taken place, as it was once surrounded by sand, but today stands on the emerald green of the lawn – the wish of the present owner, as much for practical reasons of upkeep as for beauty. A further basin beyond, profiled by a group of *putti* and dolphin, was added to the park in the nineteenth century. Now statues decorate the lateral avenues leading off the vast esplanade. The parterre in the shape of the

OVERLEAF Swans and statues are reflected in the still waters of Courances.

cross of St Andrew was transformed into a picturesque garden in 1873 and has now been restored by a new plan: above a charming statue by Poirier, made for Marly, a half reclining bather presides over yet another '*pièce d'eau*', a half moon set in a curving verdant hoop.

Returning towards the park's exit, you discover a secret garden in front of La Foulerie, a building once used to soak flax. A Japanese garden of the style popular in the great English parks of the nineteenth century was created by the Marquise de Ganay, the present owner's grandmother, to continue the water tradition of Courances. On the undulating banks of a natural pond, herbaceous and perennial plants assure continual flowering through the spring and summer. An island in the centre of the pond is exquisitely planted with a variety of Japanese maples, bamboo, azaleas and weeping willows for exotic autumn colour.

Although the Marquis de Ganay has been Mayor of Courances and *Conseiller Général* of the Essonne for thirty-five years, he is above all a man of agriculture, by training and personal inclination. This is reflected in the high standards maintained at Courances. Lawns are perfectly kept, borders filled, and the canals and basins cleared and cleaned. The waters of Courances are as pure as ever, so pure that there is now a trout hatchery. The glories of the eighteenth century have been recaptured in the twentieth.

Château des Boulayes

Tournan-en-Brie
(Madame Bouboulis)

SOME THIRTY MILES east of Paris the main road veers towards the village of Tournan-en-Brie: from the bend in the road a long avenue of plane trees leads to the Château des Boulayes, a beautiful and pure example of classical French architecture, now the property of the Bouboulis family.

The archives of Les Boulayes were destroyed during the French Revolution. All we know of the origin of the present château is that it was built in 1785 by an architect named Girardin for Claude de Ballanger, a colonel in Louis XVI's Guards, who used the land for hunting. The name of the château obviously derives from the many birch trees (*bouleaux*) that grew on the property.

The château is surrounded by an unusual moat composed of square ornamental ponds. The approach from the park and gardens used to be over a drawbridge. Bordering one side of the moat, a balustrade covered in dark ivy forms a contrast with the roses trained over the outer bank. Two *parterres à la française* stretch behind and in front of the château, a simple harmonious classical design of clipped box, flowers, grass and gravel. Avenues of pollarded limes, planted in alternate rows and clipped twice a year, close the view beyond the formal French gardens. The first pruning keeps their side branches neatly even, while the second controls growth and height. This twice-yearly pruning serves a dual purpose, both aesthetic and practical; as they are never allowed to flower, the trees' growth is thicker and more compact.

The most interesting garden at Les Boulayes is hidden behind the high walls and elegant wrought-iron gates of the old kitchen garden.

The avenue of alternate rows of lime trees was planted in 1745, before the Henri II château was destroyed.

ABOVE A hundred-year-old clipped apple tree is a decorative element in the kitchen garden.
ABOVE CENTRE Yews and ivy border the semicircular lawn.

Here, Fanny Bouboulis has combined her love of vegetables, flowers and fruit trees to make a fascinating botanical mixture. Annuals fill the borders next to leafy cabbages, which in turn edge the peat beds of the Japanese azaleas. The area set aside for culinary herbs has a most original shape. Twenty different herbs grow in a series of individual triangular beds planted in an alternating pattern: various mints, parsley, sage, chives, fennel, lavender, tarragon, marjoram and bay, with pots of basil in summer.

Sunflowers grow in long rows, their huge heads towering over the equally spectacular artichokes. A screen of sweet peas separates a row of aubergines from a colourful mass of dahlias in summer. This form of alternate planting continues right through the garden to the greenhouse, which shelters tender plants. Hundred-year-old pear or apple trees line the main path. They have been carefully shaped by constant and meticulous pruning into lattice-work sentry boxes, where the fruit seems to hang in a multitude of small windows. Madame Bouboulis takes great care of them, and was very upset by the loss of a tree last year.

The walls of the kitchen garden are espaliered with a number of varieties of different fruit trees, including peaches, cherries and fig trees ('for their different taste and the pleasure of picking fruit over a long period', says

Madame Bouboulis), interspersed with colourful clumps of flowers. There are six different varieties of pear: William, Doyenne des Comices, Conference, Duchesse d'Angoulême, Beurrée Hardy and Passecrassanne. Ten varieties of apple ensure fruit throughout the year: Calville at Christmas, Reine des Reinettes in October, Reinette Grise and Starking in January, and Golden, Pomme d'Apis, Reinette du Mans, Louise Bonne, Boskoop and Granny Smith from January to March.

Annuals are started off in small pots before being transplanted to their various beds between the fruit trees and vegetables. The garden changes each year, with subtle alterations in the choice of annuals and rotation of the vegetables. Each spring, tulips, narcissi and crocuses flower between the rows of lettuce.

Off the kitchen garden is a walled orchard where wild flowers in the long grass make a notable contrast to the tidy vegetable-flower garden. Here there are more cherry, apple and pear trees, with hazel trees, gooseberry bushes and a strawberry bed.

There is an essential difference between Les Boulayes and other gardens: most gardens are designed primarily to please the eye, while at Les Boulayes the garden was created to be eaten, but at the same time to be as attractive as possible.

Morning glories growing out of the greenhouse.

Houville-la-Branche

Auneau, near Chartres
(La Baronne de Nervo)

A charming rustic bridge over one of the many streams in the park.

HOUVILLE-LA-BRANCHE stands on the edge of the village of Auneau in La Beauce, and takes its name from the stream flowing through this most romantic of gardens.

When Madame de Nervo acquired the property in 1956, the château was set in 125 acres of forest – the last oasis of green shade before the vast and rolling plain of wheatfields that sweeps down towards Chartres. In spite of the size and elegance of the seventeenth-century château, there were no gardens to complement the noble façades. The château stood on an immense grassy meadow bordered by full-grown limes and oaks and stretching to the horizon of golden wheat.

The lie of the land imposed a natural handicap on the creation of a garden. The shady trees and open glades on the flat humid ground to the right of the château became a promenade garden. Winding paths through the woods, wide sunny avenues, water-side tracks and romantic bridges spanning the streams all invite the visitor to wander at will.

The first step was to clear away a good number of the trees in order to create vistas, while at the same time preserving groves as interesting focal points for special planting: a difficult task carried out with considerable skill. During the lengthy period of thinning out, Madame de Nervo discovered that most of the land was permanently humid. She was advised to dig a drainage system, but rejected this logical solution and instead took advantage of the nature of the terrain. The woods were full of natural springs, as well as the meandering river Branche, and these would feed future pools and ponds. In addition, there was an area ideally suited to become a bog garden – very much a rarity in France. Now, under the half-

RIGHT A majestic avenue
of poplars leads to a
romantic pool surrounded
by weeping willows.
BELOW Unexpected
sculpture on a woodland
path.

shade of a wood, a colony of *Hosta sieboldiana* mixed with other varieties, *Iris kaempferi*, astilbe, marsh marigolds and the bright yellow summer-flowering *Lysimachia punctata* provide a wide variety of colour throughout the spring and summer. Visitors are amazed by the range of plants flowering in the shade.

A path traces the course of the Branche throughout the park. Primulas, iris and climbing roses scramble haphazardly over the river banks, giving an effect of spontaneity which in fact is the result of carefully contrived and expert placing of chosen plants.

But without doubt the glory of Houville is the abundance and variety of its spring-flowering trees: Japanese cherries, amelanchier, double hawthorns, Judas trees, brooms, *Viburnum carlesii* and *Viburnum mariesi*. These

ABOVE CENTRE A group of gunnera, iris and hostas growing by the water.
ABOVE A glade filled with dwarf conifers, ferns and rocks.
LEFT The immense grassy meadow is bordered by mature limes and oaks.

Dappled sunlight through the poplar avenue.

bloom successively along a deep, grassy vista, and are discreetly mixed with a few old-fashioned roses and perennials such as delphiniums, planted informally so as to avoid any suggestion of a traditional border.

The only formal planting in this romantic garden is the curved border near the château, which in summer glows with superb standard fuchsias, fully five feet high. Each winter they are repotted and returned to the cool greenhouse for protection. Large groups of rhododendrons and azaleas are planted in the acid soil, defining the angles of the lawn and lending a splash of colour to the view from the salon windows.

Even the unexpected has its place in the garden: behind a turn in the moss-covered sandy path and partially hidden between rocks hides a strange group of gnomes, shaped in box. These mysterious genii of the garden sprang from the natural shape of the box, aided only by a little inspiration from the pruner.

A summer dahlia bed, bordered with nepeta, adds an unexpected note to the garden, an anachronistic touch of civilization. The sudden colour seems a calculated shock in this un-structured, informal garden.

A majestic avenue of poplars forms the main walk, with each tree clearly defined to create a colonnaded effect. It leads to a romantic pool encircled by weeping willows, where wild ducks mingle with decorative Chinese mandarins, swans and moorhens.

Close to the château, just before you reach the poplar avenue, Madame de Nervo shows off her spectacular planting of *Gunnera manicata*: twenty-odd giant plants grouped together, their leaves often as much as seven feet across. Other plants grow near these colossi, especially hemerocallis, with their fine, sword-like leaves. Every winter the precious gunneras are completely covered, first with their own luxuriant growth, then with a layer of dry autumn leaves held in place with wire netting, and over it all a plastic sheet to protect them from water and seasonal frosts, for despite their abundance in European summers, they are natives of the Brazilian Amazon. Every gardener has a favourite part of the garden, and this shaded valley of gunneras is Madame de Nervo's main pride and joy.

La Mormaire

near Houdan
(Monsieur Gordon Turner)

FROM 1609, a succession of owners, most of them in the king's service, lived at the château of La Mormaire on the edge of the forest of Rambouillet, once a royal hunting forest. As with so many seventeenth-century châteaux, the architectural work is unattributed; we can trace its past and imagine its history only through the etymology of its name. Trustworthy chronicles of the period mention documents in which the plot of land, and later the estate, were referred to as *Mortmer* (Dead Sea), conjuring up the image of a damp and swampy site. The broad, deep moats might have had their origin in the need to drain the land.

It was only when Gordon Turner came to live at La Mormaire in 1952 that the work of creating a garden at last began, with the help of Charles Niepce, whose extensive knowledge of botany was equalled by his love of plants. The site was very exposed, so the first priority was to provide protection from the wind by planting small hornbeams (*Carpinus*) and yews, which in time would grow into architectural windbreaks. Now, thirty years later they have reached maturity, and they represent a synthesis of three great European garden traditions: English, French and Italian – romantic, geometrical and ornate.

A flight of white doves greets visitors on arrival, and the double-level lawn bordering the main drive is the first of many visual delights. The effect has been achieved by mowing the grass closely for ten feet on either side, and leaving the rest to grow longer.

The portal and the courtyard walls that join the main building to the two wings of the château are capped with a collection of strangely baroque-looking ball-like shapes carved in sandstone. The stone very probably came from

Twin topiary pyramids mark an opening in the garden.

The freely-planted box-bordered pool walk.

a quarry at Gallardon, on the road to Chartres.

In summer a collection of orange trees, clipped into spheres and classically planted in *caissons de Versailles*, are brought out to adorn the courtyard. Pyracanthas are trained and clipped as columns against the walls of the two wings housing the library and chapel, while large pots of artemisias stand on the main steps.

There are three separate gardens, each carefully separated from the others. On the left of the main courtyard is the kitchen garden, *le potager*, encased between a broad moat, its grassy banks planted with rugosa and moss roses, and a garden wall palisaded with alternate *Magnolia grandiflora*, wisteria and ceanothus, with clematis climbing among them. A row of greenhouses is used for pot plants for

the house, with one reserved for vines, which bear the most delicious grapes. A charming grotto with lichens and small ferns adds a nostalgically rustic note. Flowers for cutting are not grown in long dull drills but instead spill out of large lavender- or box-edged squares. One square is filled with peonies and iris and a few Queen Elizabeth roses; another is planted with onopordons (thistle flowers) and thriving red and white *Nicotiana alata*, while the orange lanterns of physalis brighten the autumn scene; another square is full of roses, and elsewhere a mass of cheiranthus and *Lychnis coronaria* overflow from their enclosure. A variety of plants, including *Pulmonaria saccharata*, *Stachys lanata* and hosta, are grown as ground cover to discourage weeds. Although

this is the kitchen garden, flowers rather than leeks catch and hold the eye; while its most attractive element, which differentiates it from any other cutting and vegetable garden, is the spectacular topiary – a splendid row of green sculpture three metres high and clipped to form seven tiers standing on a green platform.

The second garden at La Mormaire lies beyond the western extension of the house, bounded by majestic walls of hornbeam and yew. Before descending into these green en-closures, pause on the terrace to admire the newest acquisition, a collection of fuchsias. Long considered too old-fashioned to be given a place in most gardens, these Victorian favourites are once more becoming popular, as the many new varieties from Central America

testify. Among the loveliest of the hybrids are 'Flying Cloud', 'Sonata', 'Bountiful', with large pink double petals and pink-veined sepals, and 'Queen May', a rustic shrubby variety with large rose petals and purple sepals. Perhaps the most beautiful of all is the pure white 'Ting-a-ling'.

Flights of steps create different levels down to the monumental walls of hornbeam pierced by long, narrow windows, an architectural wonder which is probably of Roman inspir-ation. After crossing a small terrace decorated with stone busts, a view of the central path is laid out beneath you. A pool, its edge outlined with box, stands in the centre of a lawn surrounded by box-edged beds. One contains blue- and grey-flowering plants – artemisias,

The tree-framed main lawn.

The topiary at La Mormaire: an extraordinary variety of shapes and textures.

echinops, blue aconites, agapanthus, delphiniums and palest yellow-flowering potentillas. A bouquet of pearly mauve *Salvia turkistanica*, white nicotiana, evening-fragrant hesperis, senecios, the summer-flowering geranium 'Johnson's Blue', and the ravishing paper-white tree poppy *Romneya coulteri* fill another bed. Cushions of clipped box mark the corners of each bed, underlining the formality of the design and enhancing the airy grace of the plants.

On a higher level, slightly to the left, a sundial of English design marks the centre of a small lawn, one side of which forms a slope for dry-soil-loving plants: dianthus, *Chrysanthemum haradjanii* with filigree silver foliage, heathers, sun-loving anaphalis and helianthemums.

The garden then spreads out to encompass a long vista, punctuated by high, imposing topiary pyramids. Halfway down the border a carefully placed silvery-blue cedar, *Cedrus atlantica* 'Glauca', softens the rigid severity of the design and affords colour contrast. Its branches form a silvery green canopy above the spheres, cones and pyramids of yew, and together they are a striking image of the talents of man allied with the grace of nature. A large double border of old-fashioned shrub roses flanks the grass walk, heavily scented in June when the branches are laden with blooms. Their names evoke the past: deep violet-red 'Cardinal de Richelieu', the tender rose damask 'Jacques Cartier', recurrent peony-flowering 'Paul Néron', scarlet 'Baron Girod de l'Ain', the lilac-pink-streaked 'Gros Provins Panache', the hybrid rugosa 'Blanc Double de Coubert', the excellent white 'Nevada', pale pink 'Cuisse de Nymphe Emue' and 'Souvenir de la Malmaison', the highly perfumed sugar-pink bourbon.

A few day lilies grow among the robust disease-free shrub roses, along with bergenias – useful for ground cover – and a few groups of artemisias and geraniums, and here and there long borders are edged with *Stachys lanata*.

Halfway down the rose border, surrounded by a box hedge punctuated with imposing geometrical topiary work, stands the blue cedar. The last fifty yards of the garden are planted alternately with Italian cypresses and clipped box. Beyond, a wrought-iron gate separates the garden from a rural landscape of fields and grazing cows.

OPPOSITE High, dramatic yew hedges with long narrow openings frame the entrance to the flower garden.

The third garden is the newest creation at La Mormaire, and will become the shrub garden, as imagined by Charles Niepce. It has already been planted with trees of contrasting foliage: a *Prunus sargentii*, perhaps the loveliest of all the cherries, a purple beech, another *Cedrus atlantica* and a tall liriodendron tulip tree. All these, together with variegated hollies and old chestnut trees reflect their shape and colour in the water of the surrounding moats. On the grassy bank grow majestic *Gunnera manicata* and a collection of roses that romanticize the mood of the garden: the exceptionally long-flowering white floribunda 'Iceberg', 'Golden Showers'; 'Albéric Barbier', its graceful branches covered with pale lemon-yellow flowers, a clump of the vigorous species rose *R. longicuspis*, and the hybrid musk rose 'Penelope', near which various shrubs have also been planted – laurels, escalonias and the powder-blue ceanothus 'Gloire de Versailles'.

Beyond the château towards the south-west stretches a vast lawn over 300 yards long. This serene and stately landscape, framed by the trees in the park and broken only by an ornamental stone urn at its far end, is another example of the way in which each view from the château has been planned, designed and planted to the best possible effect.

One last curious detail at La Mormaire: in the middle of a glade from which radiate the shady avenues of the park lies a gigantic lime tree. Toppled during a storm, it has grown new shoots that have been clipped into an enormous sphere. It is a living example of how a major calamity, the fall of a stately tree, can become a thing of interest and beauty through the imaginative care of a garden-lover.

A bed of white and silver plants bordered in clipped box, with a vista glimpsed through the yew hedge.

OPPOSITE ABOVE The sundial garden in its theatre of dark yews. OPPOSITE BELOW A wrought-iron gate separates the highly stylized garden from the natural landscape beyond.

Abbaye de l'Eau

near Chartres
(Monsieur et Madame François Pereire)

IN 1226, Isabelle, Countess of Chartres, founded a Cistercian abbey in the parish of Saint Victor-de-Var, nearly four miles from Chartres. The abbey survived until 1792. The French Revolution forced the sisters to abandon their convent, later sold along with all its lands and outbuildings. The following description of the abbey is drawn from an old document: 'The nearness to Chartres, the solitude of the place, vast, wooded, and enhanced by the meanderings of two serpentine rivers playing between one hundred century-old trees, predestined this ground to become a heavenly abode.' This is the place I fell in love with.

The abbey sat ceremoniously on a gravelled surface, like most French houses, and was surrounded by a few fine trees. The south façade gave on to a gentle slope leading down to the river Eure, which encircles a small island. There was no garden in 1972, the year we bought it, but there were two major attractions – the water and part of the twelfth-century cloister, miraculously preserved from destruction. A slender, carved stone colonnade framed the open arches, while mysterious steps were hidden in the thickness of the wall of the former belfry – all this made us long to make a new life for the Abbaye de l'Eau.

The visitor's first view is of the north façade of the house, massed with a group of hydrangeas harmonizing with the soft pink of the walls, a colour typical of the old houses of Chartres

A collection of topiary – square, round and pyramid-shaped yews growing on the lawn, green on green – gives formality to the

Part of the abbey ruins on the small island in the curve of the river Eure between the lawn and the meadow on the further bank.

RIGHT An urn fills the centre of this small square quiet garden surrounded by yew hedges.
FAR RIGHT Yuccas, delphiniums and foxgloves form a blue and white composition.
OPPOSITE The house viewed through an archway of exuberant 'Kiftsgate' roses, which cover the bridge to the island in June.

entrance to the house. On the southern side a double lawn terrace is underlined by a mixed evergreen border. Lavender, round cushions of summer- and winter-flowering heathers, elaeagnus, santolinas, phlomis, salvias, senecios and the marvellous cheiranthus 'Bowles variety', covered with violet flowers most of the year, ensure permanent interest. A double planting of *Pyrus salicifolia* 'Pendula' leads from the terrace to the water's edge. These graceful, slender, silver-leaved trees are underplanted with rosemary, lavender, the white-flowering veronica, *Hebe albicans*, and pink and white spring-flowering tulips. The pyrus avenue divides the garden in two.

To the right stands a seven-foot-high 'sentry box', with a domed roof, door and window, shaped in evergreen thuyas. Further down, the border becomes a scene of white, silver and yellow, with clumps of potentillas, aquilegias, achilleas, eremerus, *Lychnis coronaria* (the white-flowering campion), yellow lupins, silver santolina clipped into spheres and *Alstrœmeria litgu* interspersed with clumps of ruta. I could not resist the temptation to make a

peat bed behind these borders in order to plant a few camellias, pieris, rhododendrons, and the enchanting azalea 'Blue Tit'. Clumps of digitalis and lilies seem to grow naturally between large trees. The rose 'Kiftsgate' has climbed into a tall pine tree, from which it cascades like a bridal veil. A small artificial stream runs through this narrow woodland garden, a home to colonies of primulas, astilbes, hostas and hellebores, half-hidden under a mass of ground-cover plants: ajuga, lamium, *Phlox subulata* and pachysandra. Beyond a turn in the path four standard 'Mme Laperrière' roses grow round a central paved platform. Red rock roses grow through the cracks. In spring four beds of flaming red tulips fill this small green room with colour.

A pergola runs alongside the pyrus avenue to the east, overgrown with a tangled mixture of climbing plants: clematis, honeysuckles and roses. The most charming of these is the old rose 'Cuisse de Nymphe Emue', its name as enchanting as its breathtaking fragrance. The pergola ends at the bridge leading to a meadow planted with clumps of birches. In spring it

Crane's-bill and other perennials spill over the broad stone steps.

flowering, spreading *Lamium maculatum* 'Roseum'.

A twelfth-century chapter-house with slender columns and arched openings runs the full length of the left side of the garden. A small terrace garden, where bushes of honeysuckle are grown as standards with round clipped heads, leads to the swimming pool in front of the cloister. The pool is a simple mirror of water: neither mosaics nor sophisticated stone patterns destroy its tranquillity. The terrace is paved with old stones, while 'Iceberg' roses and large clumps of phlomis, the Jerusalem sage, blend happily with the stone retaining wall. 'Iceberg' roses, rosemary, lavender and iberis grow out of a few square openings in the pavement. A group of 'Nevada' shrub roses frames a stone bench to hide the pool from the rest of the garden.

Broad stone steps planted with *Cotoneaster horizontalis*, *Alchemilla mollis* and geranium 'Johnson's Blue' lead from the pool up to the house. My delphiniums – the blue varieties, some over six feet high – grow to the left of the steps. I refer to them as 'my' delphiniums as I am particularly proud of them. Grown from seed bought from Blackmore and Langdon, they are dead-headed after the first flowering, and then have a second flush which often lasts through October and into November. They grow in a bed of pink-flowering perennials: *Geranium endressii* flower here most of the summer, while tree mallows grow up to six feet tall next to towering hollyhocks, pink erigerons, crab apples and a wisteria trained to form a standard tree.

One of the characteristics of the garden is that the dominant colour scheme changes with the seasons. In spring, the garden wakes up with golden sunny colours; in summer, pinks and blues soften the total impression, with white bouquets; and in autumn there is a riot of blues, violets and cerise, owing to the presence in almost every border of members of the aster family. Nor is the garden empty in winter; on the contrary, it is very colourful, thanks to the golden, perfumed hamamelis, winter jasmine, the attractive *Helleborus corsicus* and *H. niger*, as well as the lovely winter-flowering heather, mahonias, skimmias, and kalmias, all of which add to the joy and colour of a winter garden.

looks like a medieval tapestry, with thousands of jonquils, narcissi, muscaris, and wild lupins growing naturally in the grass. Paths have been created by simply mowing through high grass to form a walk by the edge of the water. As this branch of the river Eure flows through the grounds it makes a large loop to encircle an island where the ruins of an old abbey building are smothered in clematis and the pearly pink rose 'New Dawn', lending it a romantic secrecy. Two topiary swans in clipped yew at the edge of the water gaze across at the real swans gliding down the river. A small wooden bridge covered with the exuberant 'Kiftsgate' rose joins the island to the garden, where a traditional long border of perennials is planted with delphiniums, irises, peonies, phlox and a variety of flowering shrubs as well as old-fashioned roses, including 'Mme Isaac Pereire' in memory of my husband's great grandmother. A round iron structure at the end of the bed is covered with small white- and mauve-flowering roses – 'Marie Odier' and 'Weichenblau' (Gertrude Jekyll's idea) – underplanted with the nettle-like, pink-

The garden is laid out on three levels. A topiary swan in clipped yew duplicates the swans on the river below.

A lush, shady planting of delphiniums and wisteria.

Château de la Celle-les-Bordes

Dampierre-en-Yvelines
(Le Duc et la Duchesse de Brissac)

LA CELLE-LES-BORDES lies within the vast forest of Rambouillet. The architecture of the château, built in 1610, is pure Henri IV, the same style as the beautiful Place des Vosges in Paris. Built by a powerful seventeenth-century noble, Claude de Harville, Marquis de Plaiseau, it remained the property of the Harvilles until it was bought in 1870 by the Duc d'Uzès, who already owned extensive lands nearby in the forest, where he was master of his own hunt. Surprisingly, La Celle-les-Bordes was bought to lodge the Duke's huntsmen and horses and to provide kennels for a pack of staghounds, while he continued to live at his own château of Bonnelles. After his death in 1878, his wife became master of the hunt. The Duc de Brissac, her grandson, inherited the property at her death in 1933.

The originality of its architecture and its astonishing interior decoration (admired by Queen Elizabeth the Queen Mother during her visit to the château in 1982) make La Celle-les-Bordes unique. The walls and beamed ceilings are decorated with 2,400 pairs of antlers – an astounding accumulation of trophies from hunts in the forest of Rambouillet.

The gardens are enchanting, and very different from anything one would expect to find

RIGHT The château behind its massive hedge. OPPOSITE Buttresses of yew are planted with a profusion of low-growing plants.

around a typically French seventeenth-century château. Designed by the Duchesse de Brissac and her second son Gilles, they are a combination of the exuberantly romantic and the rigorously formal. Gilles de Brissac spent part of his youth in England. On his return to La Celle-les-Bordes he was struck by the bareness of the area surrounding the château. He had acquired the English love of lawns, therefore a lawn was designed and planted: it would be the central feature of the future gardens, stretching up to the château, plain and simple, an echo of the garden landscapes the sixteen-year-old youth had admired on the other side of the Channel.

The gardens spread out over the different ground levels that radiate from the 650-foot-square stretch of impeccably kept lawn, bordered with the excellent red rose 'Joseph Guy'. The view has an extremely satisfying measured formality, yet a closer look reveals the conscious art behind the apparent simplicity of the scene.

In the area extending to the left-hand side of the lawn, trees have been planted as a woodland garden, mainly oaks and birches underplanted with a rich variety of shrubs and bushes: azaleas, camellias, andromedas, *Hamamelis mollis* and *Osmanthus delavayi* find a natural wooded setting. Ornamental trees and evergreens also enrich the original vegetation: *Amelanchier laevis*, the striking, fragrant, white-flowering North American June berry, the dense bushy *Pinus mugo* and *Juniperus pfitzerana aurea*. In June, old shrub roses provide unexpected colour under the trees. This wooded slope seems a completely natural part of the forest landscape, but in fact its beauty is the result of carefully studied planting.

Gilles de Brissac's favourite part of the garden is a mysterious corner between the forest and the far end of the central lawn. There is a touch of paradise about this spot: a fountain murmurs softly above patches of damp dark green moss under the deep shade, groups of rounded box topiary (one of his passions) stand near massed old-fashioned mauve aquilegias, and a mossy green path leads into the forest. Clumps of ferns outline the silver trunks of the birch trees, and massed colour groups give a sudden impression of

luxuriant vegetation to this romantic scene. A retaining wall is thick with a variety of small shrubs and horizontally-growing plants: the strata of plant life here are comparable to the different zones in a mountain landscape. Iberis, cheiranthus, dianthus, crane's-bill and many other plants dispute possession of every crack and cranny in the stone wall.

A row of yew buttresses separates the lawn from the higher, wilder part of the garden. These open enclosures in front of a low wall are part of the *trompe-l'œil* effect used to break the monotony of the long, straight line of the lawn. The buttressed compartments are planted with a profusion of low-growing and ground-cover plants: the low, spreading *Hypericum × moserianum* 'Tricolor' with a long summer season of rich golden flowers, helianthemum, rock roses, the perennial *Euphorbia polychroma*, the sub-shrubby *Phlox subulata*, and a number of bright botanical tulips, replaced later in the season by many annuals, including verbena, *Phlox drummondii* and petunias.

Gilles de Brissac has his own particular method of spotting flaws in his garden: he takes photographs of the different scenes, then, working directly on to the developed pictures, he blots out offending subjects and adds new varieties. 'I spend my time tidying up. By nature, I am an interventionist. Nature provides us a rough sketch to be improved upon and perfected', he says, reminding one of the story of the inquisitive man who asked the painter Hubert Robert why he had added a non-existent tree to a landscape painting. The answer was brief: 'It should have been there'.

The opposite side of the lawn is framed by a hedge of hornbeams, the design of which was inspired by an engraving of a ballroom in the Trianon palace at Versailles in the seventeenth century. The rigidity of the clipped hornbeams gives just the right impression of classicism. Windows have been cut into the hedge in such a way that each opens obliquely on to the valley. A direct view of the distant countryside is thus avoided and each opening frames a series of different views. A flight of steps cut through the hedge leads down to a swimming pool, surrounded by tall green walls of yew: a topiary work of great beauty and precision inspired by the gardens of the Italian

FAR LEFT Windows cut obliquely into the hornbeam hedge give a series of different views of the countryside.
LEFT Gilles de Brissac's favourite part of the garden, a mysterious corner at the far end of the lawn.

Renaissance. The retaining wall on the southern side, behind the hedged pool, forms a suntrap, crowned in summer with fat cushions of lavender, Hidcote variety hypericums and the prolific self-seeding valeriana.

Scent is very important at La Celle-les-Bordes. In every season there is at least one part of the garden specially planted for perfume. Rosemary, lavender, sage, thyme and mint – the best aromatic plants that give off their essential oils when crushed – all have their place. Other plants are so strongly scented that they perfume the air for a hundred feet around them. Spring brings daphnes, narcissi, *Viburnum carlesii*, lilacs, the scented azaleas and arborescent peonies. Roses and philadelphus, the irreplaceable mock-orange, perfume the gardens in June, while summer brings sweetly scented stock, the distinctive fragrance of heliotrope and, at night, the strong scent of white-flowering nicotiana. The garden is fragrant even in winter: the highly perfumed *Chimonanthus praecox* blooms from November to March, together with the spidery-flowered *Hamamelis mollis*; both are invaluable shrubs for the winter garden.

Above all, mention must be made of the old shrub roses which are slowly coming back into favour in France. Now, even non-specialized nurseries offer 'Cuisse de Nymphe Emue', better known in English as 'Maiden's Blush', dear to Colette in her garden. The dark-purple 'Cardinal de Richelieu' is a notable old rose, as is the deep pink *Rosa × centifolia* 'Cristata', known in France as 'Chapeau de Napoleon', because of the crested wings to the calyx that give the buds the shape of Napoleon's tricorn hat.

Colour is used lavishly everywhere – mixed freely, apparently irrespective of colour groups. The bedding-out, however, is calculated to avoid any clashes: when two

The view of the village
church from the higher
wooded part of the
garden, which in May is
carpeted with bluebells.

reds are used together, you can be sure that their flowering seasons are different and that they have been carefully placed in order to avoid too strong a colour contrast. White-flowering and foliage plants, both silver-leaved and green, set off the multi-coloured effect. There is a general feeling of ease and comfort for the plants; the whole planting scheme is uncramped, and each plant is given a generous amount of space. Wandering around La Celle-les-Bordes, you are very much aware of the harmony and balance that characterize this most unusual garden.

The immaculate lawn with the hedge of hornbeams to the right.

Château d'Anet

near Houdan

(Monsieur et Madame de Yturbe)

BUILT BY HENRI II as a gift for his beloved mistress, Diane de Poitiers, Anet is a jewel of the French Renaissance. After the strong Italian influence dominant in the reign of François I and prolonged by Catherine de Medici, it was the first great building to be designed by a French architect and built by French craftsmen. The groundwork was begun in 1547 by Philibert de l'Orme: a dry moat was dug, as well as a vast cellar, underground corridors and a drainage system. Earth from the excavations was used to build up the banks of the river Eure and to lay the foundations for the gardens, and a solid retaining wall was constructed before work could begin on the château and its grounds.

When Henri II and Diane de Poitiers arrived at Anet in 1549, the château was finished. The new building overlooked magnificent gardens, laid out in orderly horizontal lines and planes and crowned with the royal forests, the whole ensemble beautifully adapted to the structure of the site. So impressed was the King by its nobility and novelty that he stopped the work in progress on the Louvre, demolished what had already been done, and had the palace rebuilt in the new style.

The *portail* at Anet was a fitting introduction to the splendid house and gardens. A triumphal arch for Diane de Poitiers, it was crowned with a mighty stag and two hounds and on its tympan had a bronze nymph designed by Cellini, orginally for Fontainebleau. Philibert de l'Orme continued the architecture of the château into the garden. He backed the mighty retaining wall with a long vaulted gallery, supported by columns. The gallery was a device often used in the sixteenth century, providing an agreeable place to walk in all seasons. It was derived from the Roman atrium, but in a colder climate was moved from the centre of the house to enclose the gardens. At Anet the gallery was vaulted and lit by large double open windows. The exterior had a rustic air, in contrast to the magnificence of the interior, with its mosaic pavement of three colours constructed from flagstones, bricks, decorative small stones and '*paves en grès*'. Some twelve years ago a section of this pavement was discovered under the grass by a gardener, and it remains a witness to past splendour. The gallery ended in two '*culs-de-fours*' (spherical vaults), where a large marble basin was provided for Diane's nightly cold-water beauty baths. This '*cryptoportique*', as it was called, formed the fourth wall of a cloister enclosing the Renaissance garden. A grandiose, crescent-shaped double staircase leads down from the château's lower terrace to the garden.

The large Renaissance garden enclosed within the gallery formed a parterre divided into twenty-four large but unequal squares, making five paths crossed lengthways by a further three. The gallery opened on to each of these walks, and two large white marble fountains by Jean Goujon stood in the centre of the rectangle. Each square had its own planting scheme, formed by straight lines and arabesques of grass, aromatic plants and the most popular flowers of the time: violets, jonquils, lilies-of-the-valley, jasmine and stock. An extract from Clément Marot's *Le Temple de Cupide* (1515) gives a fair idea of the range:

Daisies, lilies and pinks,
Amaranthus, perfumed roses,
Rosemary, ranunculus
Fragrant lavender...
All other flowers
Throwing their soft scents
Which never trouble the heart...

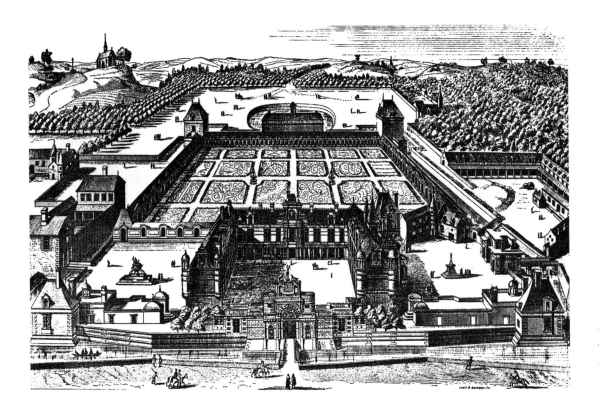

An engraving of the château shows the enclosed Renaissance garden designed by Philibert de l'Orme for Diane de Poitiers.

The chapel, part of the original construction, was decorated by Jean Goujon in 1552.

Directly behind the enclosed garden and gallery a vast empty lawn held an artificial lake, large enough to stage water fêtes and naval battles against sea monsters for the amusement of the King and Court. Towards the main garden and lake, the park was divided into numerous compartments, some planted with fruit trees, others miniature meadows starred with wild flowers and watered by brooks, while others held ornamental trees. These were clipped into spheres, flat parasols, pyramids, and even hollow crowns, and stood on a series of steps which formed flowered mosaic pedestals, each planted with flowers of one colour. Canals encircled islands and tame deer wandered free under the large trees in the wooded enclosures. Traditionally, one deer wore a silver collar inscribed *Dianae me vovit Henricus* (I am consecrated to Diane by Henri). Anet was a magnificent gift from Henri II to his mistress; but it was Diane de Poitiers who made it a French paradise of endless pleasures and inventions to hold and enchant the King.

When Diane de Poitiers' grandson, Charles de Lorraine, Duc d'Aumale, inherited Anet in 1576, garden history was made. D'Aumale placed Anet and all his other châteaux in the charge of Etienne Dupeyrac, later Henri IV's chief architect, who, like so many other Frenchmen, had been greatly influenced by his travels in Italy. The very year of his return he published his *Vues Perspectives des Jardins de Tivoli*, his own attitudes radically changed by that first shock of discovery in Italy. No longer did he see a garden as an assortment and accumulation of small unrelated plots; now he conceived of it as a whole, and at Anet designed France's first parterres and compartments '*en broderie*'. He placed the maintenance of the garden in the hands of young Claude Mollet, whose father, the founder of this great French family of gardeners, had worked at Anet before becoming the royal gardener at the Tuileries. Until that time French gardeners had had no part in the designing of gardens and hardly any choice in planting schemes. They were workmen, following orders as best they could in gardens created by architects.

Claude Mollet was the first to change this. In later life he described his difficulties in maintaining Dupeyrac's embroidery patterns at Anet: the green plants were simply not hardy enough to stand the cold winters and hot summers of the Ile de France; plant loss was heavy and the resulting labour problems enormous. Mollet's eventual solution was to use box to keep the designs green: in his words, box was a novelty, and unpopular at the time. The rest of the story has become gardening history. Henri IV, impressed by the success of Mollet's new style of garden design, commissioned him to create the gardens at St-Germain-en-Laye, Fontainebleau and

ABOVE This much admired double hemicycle flight of steps leads to the lovely Renaissance side garden.

ABOVE RIGHT Philibert de l'Orme's *cryptoportique* formed the first side of the original enclosed garden. Diane de Poitiers bathed nightly in cold water to preserve her beauty in the vast marble bath that still stands sheltered under the right-hand *portique*.

Monceau. In 1630 Mollet succeeded his father at the Tuileries. The new style was quickly imitated, and spread to the rest of Europe – encouraged by his son André's book, *Jardin de Plaisir*, published in 1651 while he was the official gardener to Queen Christina of Sweden.

The next grand, though less historic, transformation of Anet was made by Louis-Joseph de Vendôme, one of the most eccentric figures of seventeenth-century France. Reputedly, his virtues shone as brightly as his vices were base. He loved Anet, and surrounded himself there with a small but brilliant group of friends and writers who accepted his vices and eccentricities, just as he respected their freedom and lack of obsequiousness. The Dauphin's visit to Anet in 1685, prompted by the King, served as an excuse for the intensive rebuilding of the château and the redesigning of the park. A tide of demolition swept over the grounds. The Renaissance garden and park, which had fallen into disrepair, were completely transformed. The gallery and enclosed parterres might have been preserved, but instead were razed together

with many of the out-buildings. Ironically, the transformations were carried out by Le Nôtre, godson of d'Aumale's great gardener, Claude Mollet.

In 1576, when he was one of the leaders of the Holy League, an alliance with Philip II of Spain during the French Wars of Religion, the Duc d'Aumale, who had to keep his troops occupied and out of trouble during that restless winter, put them to work digging a canal and enlarging the small branch of the Eure which flows near Anet. Running along the main axis of the château, the canal became Le Nôtre's focal point in the new plan for the garden. It was widened and lengthened to its present proportions, over 2,000 yards long by 200 feet wide. Avenues of lime trees were planted on each side and a low weir was added to break the flat surface of water. Lastly, stone edging created the typical seventeenth-century sense of elegance.

Meanwhile, the garden was divided into compartments planted *en broderie*, while beyond the canal a new park was laid out with avenues of trees radiating from *ronds points*. A small wood full of *cabinets de verdure* was made to mask the servants' quarters.

After the death of the Duc de Penthièvre (the last owner before the Revolution) in 1793, Anet suffered many vicissitudes: partial destruction, vandalism, pillage, even the cutting down of all its trees. Its sale in 1840 to the Comte de Caraman marked the beginning of the long restoration of the château and its park and gardens, continued during the nineteenth and twentieth centuries. In 1974, Monsieur et Madame de Yturbe, the present owners, asked Mogens Tvede, the landscape architect, to make a new plan for the old *potager*, Anet's kitchen garden. The lovely rounded back wall now rises beyond a swimming pool set in a smooth lawn. A hedge of thuyas has been planted to screen this section from the rest of the new garden. Over twenty years ago, the ancient fruit trees were stripped from the beautiful pink and yellow lichen-covered park wall in order to preserve it, and new fruit trees were planted, some to line the main side walks, and some to divide the garden into six compartments – vegetables alternating with flowers for cutting and with plants of particular interest to Madame de Yturbe. The Yturbe family patiently and lovingly continues to restore Anet, to recover its past as well as to expand its possibilities.

Although much has been lost, Anet still holds echoes of the past. In 1879, Philibert de l'Orme's '*cryptoportique*' was rediscovered and disinterred after almost 200 years. André Malraux, while Minister of Culture, returned Diane de Poitiers' tomb to her funeral chapel in 1965. The lovely small Renaissance garden near the great portal, with its much admired double-semicircular flight of steps, is again as it was when Diane de Poitiers walked there. *Liriodendron tulipifera* have replaced lime trees and reflect their autumnal gold in Le Nôtre's superb canal. The poem that Le Chevalier de Florian composed about Anet for the Duc de Penthièvre again rings true:

>Always Anet belonged
>Either to beauties or to heroes.
>Henri built its walls, monuments of
>   tenderness;
>Each stone still offers its crescent moons
>And tells us that here Diane is mistress …

LEFT The rounded wall at the end of the kitchen and cutting garden, redesigned in 1974 by Mogens Tvede. BELOW The *portail*, a fitting introduction to the splendour of Anet.

Haras de Varaville

Varaville, near Cabourg

(Le Baron et la Baronne van Zuylen)

VARAVILLE has been a stud-farm since the eighteenth century: the date carved on the wall in the stable yard is 1719. Horses were probably bred on this lime-rich land before William of Normandy won his first battle here against the French king, and before he crossed the Channel to conquer England. The eighteenth-century château, built close to the stables, was destroyed by fire in 1937, and when we bought the property in 1964, all that was left were the foundations, barely visible under the long grass of an overgrown lawn. There was a large walled kitchen garden, gone to seed, and the remnants of a broken and rusted pergola – the ghost of a vanished garden. But the heavy scent of the rugosa roses next to the crumbling walls was strong and sweet.

It would have been impossible to rebuild the château, and absurd to attempt a Norman-style travesty, so we decided, with great excitement, to raze the foundations and build a modern house.

I asked Russell Page, the eminent landscape gardener, to come and see the stud farm with me in 1966; I wanted him to design a garden and make a plan that would bridge the two-

RIGHT Spring in the predominantly white summer garden.
OPPOSITE Bluebells fill the woodland garden after the early spring-flowering bulbs have finished.

RIGHT Plants spill over the central brick path in the summer garden.
BELOW White lupins in the front of the summer garden.
OPPOSITE ABOVE *Stachys lanata* edges the border in the rose garden.
OPPOSITE BELOW Mixed clematis growing over the espaliered pear trees on the long stone wall in the back garden.

hundred-year architectural gap between the existing farm buildings and the future modern house. The house was to be built on two levels, so that from the glassed-in living room and terrace we could see the horses in the paddocks behind the end wall of the garden. The view would be superb, but the house, already a doubtful addition to the Norman landscape, would have to be perched on top of a mound of earth and rubble left over from the old château.

Russell Page was somewhat hesitant before agreeing to try to resolve the difficulties and design the garden. Modern architecture, particularly in private houses, is a rarity in rural France, and is both disliked and mistrusted. It would be difficult to relate such a house to the older structures of the stud-farm and walled garden. Our friend Peter Harnden, an American architect, concentrated on the plan of the house, built in the same stone as the stable buildings: the yellowish Caen stone (brought to England by William the Conqueror to build the first Tower of London, and later some of the English cathedrals). Russell Page's role would be more complex and exacting: to reconcile the architectural differences by means of the garden, and to make the steepish banks between the house and ground level acceptable. The existing slope would have ended against the front wall of the kitchen garden, a visual absurdity. Russell Page's solution was to open the long rectangular walled garden by removing the wall nearest the house, and then to reduce the slope of the embankment by means of a low retaining wall, which supported the paved terrace next to the house. Two simple curving flights of steps, paved in the same dark unpolished slate as the floors of the house and the terrace, would link the whole to the lawn and gardens below. The three remaining walls of the old garden would provide the framework for a series of smaller gardens, enclosed by parallel yew hedges on both sides of a central lawn. These side gardens between the yew hedge and the outer wall would be divided into three smaller compartments, or 'rooms'.

The area between the yew hedge and the outside wall on the right would be separated into three sections and planted with roses. The other side of the lawn was also planned in three sections: a central bed for annuals and a smaller area at either end for early and late herbaceous planting.

To the south of the house, where there were some large trees, we made a central lawn bounded by a low wall, beyond which stretched an avenue of beech trees. Either side of the lawn loose informal beds would be planted with white-flowering shrubs.

There is no land to spare on a stud-farm – no horseman will willingly relinquish good grass-land for the frivolous pleasures of gardening. The answer to a plea for just a little more land is 'grow anything you like on the fences, as long as it won't poison the bloodstock'. I have subsequently discovered that young horses would prefer to eat roses, no matter how thorny, than grass. So the garden had to be developed inside existing boundaries, whether walls or fences. On the embankment we deci-ded to use a wide variety of shrubs: large ones to give accent and weight, and then drifts of low-growing shrubs and suitable herbaceous and ground-cover plants. The idea was to contrast different textures, habits of growth and colours of foliage, whether deciduous or evergreen, so that the banks would be a bonus to the garden – and this too had to be worked out very carefully. The bank was divided into three sections: the south bank, facing the white shrub garden, the north slope, overlooking the orchard where yearling fillies graze, and the central area, facing west towards the lawn and the main garden.

The embankment surrounding and support-ing the house on three sides would necessarily be a focal point of the garden, to set the house in its framework of the green pastures of Basse Normandie, and soften the transition between the modern house, the formally enclosed gardens and the stone buildings of the stud-farm.

The dominant colour scheme on the south bank is blue and grey with some pink and touches of white to bring the whole effect into focus. Amongst the blues are the late summer-flowering ceanothus 'Autumnal Beauty' and 'Gloire de Versailles', planted near the pink 'Marie Simon'. They grow next to the edge of the terrace, close to some blue-flowering hibis-

White wisteria grown as a small tree, just coming into flower near the white shrub garden.

cus 'Blue Bird', which also forms a group next to a large bed of lavender. All the plant groups are generous and they are usually repeated to balance the general effect. Other blues are brought into play with the graceful *Perovskia atriplicifolia* 'Blue Spire' and *Caryopteris clandonensis*. The handsome notched leaves of white and violet-spiked acanthus lend an architectural element to the planting near the terrace, where a river of small-flowered blue agapanthus runs down and across the middle of the bank. The family cat favours a large patch of nepeta where she sits for hours, her round blue eyes on the watch for birds. Blue dwarf Michaelmas daisies prolong the colour scheme into autumn, as does *Ruta graveolens* 'Jackman's Blue', its insignificant yellow flowers pinched out to make the plant bushier, in a corner at the bottom of the bank.

The taller shrubs include a group of fragrant Persian lilacs, *Syringa persica*, which reflower lightly in August if dead-headed after Easter, and the excellent autumn-flowering *Desmodium penduliflorum* whose long, arching wands are heavy with rosy-purple pea flowers, as well as the rather tender white, late-flowering *Escallonia × iveyi*. A white wisteria grown as a standard makes a charming small tree near the bottom of the bank. Later, I added a number of cistus: two white-flowering

varieties, *C. ladaniferus* and *C. cyprius*, and the vivid purple *C. pulverulentus* next to *C.* 'Silver Pink'. *Artemisia arborescens* and *Stachys lanata* add patches of silver to the picture.

Taller shrubs are kept pruned to the height their position on the bank demands. The shaping and pruning is rather haphazard, done when I realize that they have exceeded their bounds, but all the herbaceous plants are cut hard back in early spring, and cuttings are taken regularly in summer to ensure a reserve of plants for renewing the beds. There is quite a bit of plant movement; after fourteen years, many shrubs have become too invasive, too big or simply straggly. When Russell Page comes to visit, he gently points them out. They are removed and replanted elsewhere in the garden.

On one corner of the terrace there is an excellent accidental combination of plants: rosemary flowering at the same time as the lovely pink old shrub rose, 'Gloire de Guinon', underplanted with the stiff blue-flowering *Clematis heracleifolia* 'Davidiana'.

Camellias grow on the shaded northern edge of the terrace. At the suggestion of the Vicomte de Noailles a pit was dug, lined with plastic, and filled with peat. They have survived and flourished in spite of the very alkaline soil.

On the north-facing area the colours are darker and the planting less diverse. *Juniperus horizontalis* and low-growing cotoneasters are lightened by the yellow-flowering hypericum, *Potentilla fruticosa* and *Cytisus × præcox*, as well as a group of modern shrub roses, the excellent 'Golden Wings' variety.

The western bank runs the full length of the terrace, facing the deep rectangular lawn between the yew-hedged gardens. Its length is broken by paved, stepped paths that start straight from the terrace next to the house and then curve outwards. The steps are irregularly spaced to follow the slope of the bank before joining a series of fine gravel paths that circle the bottom of the side banks and lead into the two end gardens. Two *Cupressus glabra*, planted beneath each other on the slope, help to cut the horizontal line. The rest of the bank is planted with large groups of chaenomiles, stretches of blue- and magenta-flowering crane's-bill, *Geranium magnificum* and *G. sanguineum*, junipers, the dwarf *Spiræa bumalda* and a variety of potentillas. A wild rose, *Rosa spinosissima* 'Lutea', makes an enormous impenetrable and prickly thicket – as its name indicates – on the edge of the lawn, near a bordering group of mauve-pink *Sedum spectabile*.

The layout of the main garden can clearly be seen from the terrace, but the individual gardens behind the lateral yew hedges can only be guessed at. You catch a glimpse of white roses, or a few splashes of colour below the round heads of hawthorn and crab apple trees. The composition of each smaller area remains separate and secret, in spite of their inter-connection Pink and yellow roses are planted out in four geometrical corner compositions, each in turn divided into three parts by inner hedges of lavender, and one central diamond-shaped bed. The pink and yellow rose garden is separated from the red rose garden by a lawn, deeply bordered with the white floribunda 'Iceberg'. This grass patch is divided into four squares by two crossed paths laid in brick, a pyramidal shaped yew set in each. All the inner paths in the gardens are made of brick, the outer paths covered in washed pea gravel. Climbing roses, clematis and passion flowers cover the south wall, edged with a row of small old shrub roses underplanted with beds of *Iris reticulata*, mixed bluebells, summer blooming galtonias and chives. The chives are supposed to be a natural remedy against black spot, but so far have been unsuccessful. This border is edged with silvery-grey *Stachys lanata*. The seven beds in the red rose garden are edged in box, the roses chosen primarily for their scent: 'Papa Meilland', 'Etoile de Hollande', 'Fragrant Cloud', and glowing scarlet 'Josephine Bruce'; for me, scent is almost as important as texture and colour in the garden.

The succession of small gardens on the other side of the lawn begins with the spring garden, a grassed square with a deep border of small bulbs that flower from early spring until the peonies, delphiniums and eremurus take over. Before Easter, the *Magnolia soulangeana*, its bare branches covered with tulip-shaped purple-stained flowers, is a lovely sight in the corner of the garden, and almost lovelier seen from the house over the yew hedge. Four *Rosa* 'Nevada' grow in each corner, and four violet-purple-

flowering lilacs, grown as standards, stand guard beside the two openings in the garden. In summer, *Campanula persicifolia*, *C. pyramidalis*, *C. lactiflora* and masses of violet, rose and mauve-blooming phlox fill this section.

The summer garden is planted in whites and silver with some darker green foliage plants for contrast. Occasionally another colour creeps in, sometimes on purpose, like *Lachenalia glaucina* and the almost black *Fritillaria persica* 'Adiyaman'; others quite accidentally, like the pink Japanese anemones, quickly transferred to the spring garden. These Japanese anemones are beautiful and useful, as in late summer they follow the white phlox, *Gypsophila elegans*, *Campanula persicifolia* and the white-flowering *Achillea ptarmica* 'The Pearl'. Other plants in this garden are *Achillea argentea* and *A.* 'Moonshine', and the summer hyacinth, *Galtonia candicans*. Silver foliage plants include *Artemisia nutans*, *A. purshiana* and the taller *A. ludoviciana*. Many spring bulbs have crept in over the years: *Anemone blanda* 'Alba', snowdrops with their green-rimmed bells, double white hyacinths, even some white crocuses and bearded irises. An ironwork seat stands under a silver-grey *Pyrus salicifolia* – a faint but recognizable echo of the white garden at Sissinghurst.

The two seasonal gardens are separated by a

series of box-edged squares, twenty-four in all. Russell Page's lovely idea was to grow tulips, one colour per square, to make a spring palette of contrasting and harmonizing colours. The squares would be planted with annuals in the summer. Notwithstanding the excellence of the initial idea, the reality has been a disaster: no part of the garden provokes such annual despair. The tulips never grow evenly, some squares are stripped bare by rabbits, and for years a local thief came nightly during May, at First Communion time, to cut the best flowers, until we announced in the village that a series of traps and alarms had been set throughout the garden. In summer, the situation is just as dramatic but I continue to hunt for a solution. Eight of the twenty-four squares have been filled with box, with four clipped trees to add height in the four middle squares.

The end garden is a contrast to Russell Page's formal layout. It had been reserved for a swimming pool, but after three years of hesitation I felt the need for space, particularly for the increasing number of old and modern shrub roses I longed to plant. Owing to a prolonged postal strike in England I had to go ahead on my own with no help from Russell Page. The first result was a restless series of curved beds filled with large shrub roses and flowering shrubs, with hawthorns and crab apples for height. The stone walls had already been espaliered with pears and apples, cherries and, on the south side, peaches. Many clematis have been added over the years, to the detriment of the fruit but for the beauty of the garden. In winter, the walls are underplanted with pansies and the smaller, lovelier *Viola cornuta*, in spring with white- and pink-flowering narcissus, and in summer with a 'wild' seed mixture devised and sold by Tubergen in Holland. Over the past ten years, some beds have been removed, quietening the garden, and others underplanted with drifts of white agapanthus and stately acanthus.

The other side of the long wall at the back of the end garden is covered with roses: the thornless Bourbon 'Zéphirine Drouhin' grows around the white wooden door set in the stone wall, and rugosas, including 'Roseraie de l'Hay', recovered from the old garden, are trained against the wall. Bearded irises border

the length of the warm west wall, planted in alternating colour groups of violet, blue, yellow and white, and faced by the white fences of the yearling paddock.

The entrance drive leads from the road to a paved courtyard at the back of the house, and the south lawn is enclosed by curving beds of shrubbery. Some of the planting in the beds was devised for summer: a tall mixed group of *Buddleia davidii* 'White Cloud' and 'White Profusion', and two corner groups of *Hydrangea macrophylla*, the lacecaps *H.* 'Maculata' and *H. paniculata* 'Grandiflora'. But most of the beds are planted with spring-flowering shrubs: *Choisya ternata*, *Spiræa thunbergii*, *Fatsia japonica* 'Variegata', *Magnolia stellata*, and massed *Philadelphus* × *Lemoinei*. The best white lilac, *Syringa* 'Monique Lemoine', grows behind weigela 'Mont Blanc', and one of the loveliest of the Japanese cherries, *Prunus* 'Shimidsu Sakura', yields clusters of pure white flowers. The arching hybrid musk rose 'Pax' makes a large shrub, and is particularly fine in early autumn. The viburnums too have a place in the shrub garden, especially the turquoise fruited *Viburnum davidii*, the fragrant *V.* × *burkwoodii*, followed by the later-flowering *V. carlesii* and, lastly, the elegant shade-loving *Viburnum turcatum* and lace-capped *V. plicatum* 'Mariesii'.

Perhaps the prettiest garden at Varaville is the woodland garden, planted under the grove of old trees behind the spring garden. Winter-flowering cyclamens, primroses, hellebores and hepaticas begin blooming in the grey cold of winter under the bare trees and, as more and more bulbs come into flower, the ground turns into a tapestry of snowdrops, eranthis, dark and light blue muscari, blue-white puschkinia, the graceful dog-tooth violet, erythronium, galanthus, chionodoxa and wood violets, *Fritillaria meleagris* and the curious plum-bordered yellow *F. michailovskyi* tucked between the roots of the trees. In May, the ground is carpeted with bluebells and lilies-of-the-valley, which were planted against the wall but have mysteriously moved across the path to naturalize themselves under the trees. May also brings the aquilegia and last of all the tall foxgloves. The woodland garden makes the final poetic transition between the eighteenth-century stud-farm and modern Varaville.

The rectangular central rose garden, heavily planted with the vigorous white floribunda 'Iceberg'. The modern house is just visible to the right of a white mulberry tree.

Manoir de Criqueboeuf

Bonnebosq, near Pont-l'Evêque
(Mr Yul Brynner)

BELOW The half-timbered sixteenth-century manor house flanked by two stone towers faces a broad lawn.
OPPOSITE *Gunnera manicata* fills the centre of the water garden.

CRIQUEBOEUF is amazingly difficult to find. The entrance, simple and discreet, is hidden behind a hedge of trees on the right side of the main road between Valsemé and the village of Bonnebosq. But once you are in the narrow secret lane that leads to the manor, a special charm surrounds you. In spring, the steep banks of the lane become a wilderness of celandines, violets and pale yellow primroses. Young leaves meet overhead to form a green archway, the perfect setting for a sylvan fairy tale. A sudden transition from shade to full light, and the towered manor, set behind a vast lawn, is before you. Old apple trees stand in front of it, their branches so laden with fruit by the end of the summer that they sweep the grass. The house itself, a half-timbered sixteenth-century manor, is beautifully proportioned and framed by two stone towers. From the end of the lawn one of the towers appears very slightly higher than the other, softening the severity of the architectural line. The unevenness of the roof, in saffron-coloured tiles, testifies to the age of the building. The grey stone towers and faded brownish-grey timber set in the white walls give the effect of a daguerreotype, standing in the rich green pastures of Normandy.

Little is known about the origins of the property. The earliest known seigneurs of Criqueboeuf, named Mont, can be traced to about 1378. After them, a succession of families owned the property, all bearing names well known in the Pays d'Auge – quiet names, devoid of history. Ownership of the domain filtered down through a progression of modest, local families, until, at the end of the First World War, the manor was bought by a farmer by the name of Delafosse. He kept his cows on the ground floor, hens in the bedrooms, and forage for his beasts in the two towers. Not surprisingly, Criqueboeuf remained hidden and dilapidated until 1959, when M. Jacques Abreu, a Cuban resident in France, bought the property and restored it.

In 1970, Yul Brynner and his French wife were looking for a home in Normandy. They learned that Criqueboeuf was for sale, visited it and made the transaction the same year. It was the first time that Yul Brynner had owned a house, for his nomadic past had prevented him settling anywhere permanently.

The Brynners' first concern after moving in that autumn was for the land surrounding the manor; fields had to be turned into lawns, orchards thinned to preserve only the best trees, and the whole garden replanted. First, the gravel in front of the house was replaced by grass (there is always a great reticence in France about bringing the lawn up to the house – an assumption that family and visitors will dirty the house walking in from grass). A yew hedge was planted to make a low thick wall opening out towards the view, the enclosed space was grassed and a broad path in rounded paving stones set in the new lawn. Ceanothus and lavender were mixed in beds under the towers and combined plantings of wisteria and roses were trained up the stone walls. Two bay laurels clipped into fat round balls stand on either side of the old wooden door in small white *caissons de Versailles*.

The open field in front of the manor was mown and made into a lawn, and just enough apple trees were retained to make a double row leading down to the boundary hedge of hawthorns. An old walnut tree was spared, and now, full of honeysuckle and climbing roses, still bears a heavy autumn load of nuts. In

August the nearby plum tree is laden with purple fruit. Yul Brynner placed the beautiful Japanese maple, *Acer japonicum* 'Vitifolium', near the house to delight with its brilliant autumn foliage, and Japanese flowering cherries and quinces were added for memory's sake, an echo of summers he spent as a child in Nara, the chief Buddhist centre of ancient Japan.

A still pool, or *mare*, separates Criqueboeuf from the neighbouring farm. Yul Brynner took weeping willow cuttings, planted them upside down, (an old Gypsy trick), and now they grow stiffly upright to make an excellent natural curtain. Jacques Bourgeois, the gardener, takes a less romantic view and claims they are pollarded willows cut back hard every winter to form thick nobbly heads. Jacques, who is Norman born, served as the Vicomte de Noailles' chauffeur-valet from the age of fourteen. In the course of his work, he saw all the great gardens of Ireland and England, and developed an extensive knowledge of gardening from the Vicomte, a great gentleman and gardener. He has been with Jacqueline Brynner, the Vicomte's niece by marriage, since 1963, and the gardens of Criqueboeuf have become his life's work.

The previous owners had asked Russell Page to draw up a plan for the grounds. The shape of the cutting garden was traced and an open swimming pool was dug on one side of the manor, but, incomprehensibly, the rest was never finished and the plan was sadly lost. Yul Brynner did not want a pool, and the continual bother of its upkeep; but, on the other hand, there it was and it had to be put to use, so the area was fenced, planted and grassed, and penguins were brought in to inhabit it. These acrobatic creatures made a charming but freakish addition to the landscape – comic variations on the black and white Frisian cows grazing in the neighbouring fields. (Perhaps they reminded the owner of his days as a circus acrobat, before he broke his back in a performance.) But the penguins had two severe drawbacks: they rapidly ate all the plants, aquatic or otherwise, and the enormous quantity of fish they required filled the house and garden with their aroma. They would have to go. Yul Brynner, with habitual generosity,

offered them to unwilling friends, until with regret he finally gave them to a Zoological Park at Cléry near Rouen.

Animals are not unusual at Criqueboeuf, nor is Yul Brynner's generosity. Years ago I read an article on the joy and usefulness of toads in the garden. As mine was toadless, I asked, in passing, whether there was a small surplus toad at Criqueboeuf. Six months later, I received a basket of six giant toads, *Bufo bufo amazonia*, flown in direct from Manaos. The poor unacclimatized creatures survived barely a week in the inclement, freezing Norman spring. I later learned that a similar shipment arrived at Criqueboeuf, dying after two days.

Undeterred by this episode, Mr Brynner decided to use the pool to make a tropical water garden, which has become the most inspired part of the garden. Stone was used to build up the edges of the pool, softening and breaking the classical rectangular shape. Island beds were built and the whole garden enclosed in high yew hedges. The garden is dominated by an enormous *Gunnera manicata* growing in the middle of the pool: kneeling on the grass to look at the flowering cones deep in the heart of

A small stone fountain for Yul Brynner's collection of fantail and tumbler pigeons stands in the centre of the silver and blue garden.

it is like entering a Douanier Rousseau painting. The dark kidney-shaped leaves are well over two feet long. The plant was a present from the Baronne de Nervo's garden near Chartres, a small cutting that no one, except Yul Brynner, ever believed would survive. But, it has flourished in Normandy as if it were growing in its native Brazil, triumphantly emerging each spring from its winter protection of last year's cut leaves.

The water garden is a tropical abundance of graceful slender-leaved bamboos, red-hot spiked kniphofia, superb *Yucca gloriosa*, bulrushes and masses of hemerocallis. The pool is covered with lotuses and water-lilies; small emerald green frogs, brought back from a trip to Japan, sit like jewels on the lily pads, while a hidden fountain adds the sound of water to the magic of this tropical garden in the heart of the Pays d'Auge. A very special tree, a present from Henry Fonda, grows in one corner of the garden; a dwarf Japanese maple, originally a bonsai and over 100 years old, which, left to its own devices, has astounded everyone by its vigorous growth. A rounded yew hedge partially shuts off the back of the garden and gives additional depth to the enclosure. Silver birches and a group of dogwoods were planted on the other side of this hedge; the beautiful North American *Cornus florida* has yet to flower, in spite of lavish amounts of peat added to the

soil. Yul Brynner also wanted a garden close to the house – a garden as lovely in winter as in summer, colourful even in the winter frosts. Jacqueline Brynner, inspired by photographs of Lady Iveagh's gold and silver gardens designed by Gertrude Jekyll at Pyrford in Surrey, set to work on the far side of the manor, on the site of Russell Page's unfinished rose garden. It would be a garden exclusively of foliage plants and provide colour and contrast throughout the year. The existing parallel yew hedges were extended to make an end 'room', only visible from the side of the house. The long front section is planted for a golden effect, and the far end is a composition of greys, blues and silver.

Jacques trained a series of ball-shaped yews along the top of the hedge to break the monotonous straight lines, and curving beds were added to the central carpet of grass. Four feathery *Cryptomeria* 'Elegans' were set against the dark green yews on either side of the garden and the beds filled with gold-leaved plants: *Elæagnus aurea*, golden hollies, *Elæagnus pungens* 'Maculata' with gold splashed leaves, and a border of bright yellow-tipped heather.

A stone basin stands on the axis of the silver-blue garden, further on. White fan-tailed pigeons perch on the basin to drink and preen and flutter under the slender jet of the fountain. Behind them, an archway cut in the hedge frames the drooping silhouette of a *Sequoiaden-dron pendulum*, its long branches hanging down the narrow column of the trunk. The southern archway leads to the water garden and its astounding gunnera, while the northern opening leads out towards the apple and pear orchard behind the house. Four corner beds are filled with silver-grey and blue-flowering plants: lilacs, the tall spikes of *Salvia turkista-nica*, the summer-flowering classic, *Ceanothus* 'Gloire de Versailles', silver artemisias and blue nepeta. An almost recumbent blue cedar, *Cedrus glauca pendula*, its trunk trained horiz-ontally, branches dripping to the ground, forms a curtained archway linking the gold garden to the orchard north of the manor. Yul Brynner prunes the cider apples himself, and over the years has given them slightly oriental shapes. Peat beds were made on one side of the garden hedge for plants that cannot tolerate lime. Winter-flowering heathers border islands of pieris, azaleas and sweet-scented *Viburnum fragrans*, which provide a quiet back-ground for the foamy blossoms of the pear trees in the spring.

It was fitting that the Brynners should ask M. Prévosteau, a fine horticulturalist, who had frequently collaborated with Russell Page, to give the cutting garden new life, design a kitchen garden, and provide Criqueboeuf with trees and plants.

The original plan of the cutting garden was partly retained: a rectangle, bordered on three sides by high clipped yew hedges, the neat beds filled with culinary herbs, bright dahlias, del-phiniums, herbaceous peonies, stiff zinnias and even special roses for the house. A low wire fence separates the long back of the cutting garden from a pond which houses a collection of exotic water fowl.

A half-timbered miniature garden-house covered in passion flowers makes a convenient architectural division between this and the kitchen garden. M. Prévosteau made a simple yet elegant plan for the *potager*. A broad grass path runs down the centre of the garden, lined with box-bordered rose beds, and sturdy un-painted wooden trellises covered with climb-ing roses screen off the rest of the garden. Vegetables are mixed together in the back beds: American hybrid corn near the large

decorative dahlias and small sunflowers alongside the artichokes. Pyramids of clipped yew mark the four cardinal points, and two large squares in box indicate the exact centre of the garden. Three of the four sides are modest-ly hedged with laurel, while the end wall is covered with espaliered fruit trees. Climbing 'Sonia Meilland' grows through the laurel hedge to form a rose-decked entrance archway.

Behind the kitchen garden there is a special walk, a favourite of the Brynners' two adopted Vietnamese daughters, where each year, on the first day of January, they bring their Christmas trees out to plant. And so the years are measured in happy memories in this special garden in Normandy.

ABOVE A weeping blue cedar forms a curtain between the apple and pear orchard and the gold garden.
TOP Roses growing in the cutting garden by the caretaker's cottage.

Château de Brécy

near Bayeux

(Monsieur et Madame Jacques de Lacretelle)

THIS EXTRAORDINARY GARDEN is both Baroque and Renaissance in style, and may well have been designed by François Mansart in the mid-seventeenth century. With its rising terraces and lavish use of fantastical sculpture, stone balustrades and Italianate perspectives, the sophistication and complexity of the architectural design is extraordinary.

The first surprise is the elegant portal, nearly thirty feet high, with a sculptured pediment and Ionic pilasters. The style of the house, on the other hand, is far more in keeping with the country road and simple, good stone farmhouses of the district.

But even the portal is small preparation for the wonder of the garden beyond the house, rising like a picture to the sky. You might imagine you were in the garden of an Italian *palazzo*, were it not for the black and white Frisian cows grazing in the meadow behind the lovely ironwork ornamental gate, with its tulips and acanthus leaves, at the top of the garden. Five terraces, separated by stone walls topped with balustrades, mount elegantly towards the wrought ironwork silhouetted against the ever-changing Normandy sky. They are unequal in width; the lowest level is no wider than the two indented side-rooms of the house, the second and third are fairly deep, and the fourth and fifth are quite shallow, so that the flight of steps leading from one terrace to the next appears to form an unbroken continuity.

The steps, like all the architectural devices at Brécy, merit attention. Laid on the central axis of the garden, they provide the eye with a strong vertical line in contrast to the many horizontal lines of the terraces. The first and fourth set of steps are laid straight; on the fourth level the first six steps are rounded towards the house while the upper ones curve towards the top of the garden; the steps leading to the fifth level form a pyramid; and the final set is rounded and faces back and down into the garden, artfully imposing visual limits to the total space.

While such sophistication and complexity of design and detail may seem mysterious in this rural setting, it is certainly no happy architectural accident. We know that the garden was probably begun in 1653, when the owner, François Lebas, married Catherine Roger, whose initials, together with his, are worked into the flower and leaf motifs of the ornamental gate. They probably met François Mansart and his family while he was working on the Château de Balleroy in the neighbourhood. Thirty-two years later their son, Claude Lebas, married Jules-Hardouin Mansart's daughter. Versailles' architect was François Mansart's great-nephew. All this evidence is circumstantial, but no more so than the claim that Salomon de Brosse, architect of the Palais du Luxembourg, or one of his group, designed the portal and the garden, based as it is on the negative fact that François Mansart is not known to have used segmented pediments, found here on the entrance and in two of the doors set in the garden. The attribution is a mystery, but be that as it may, tradition claims Mansart and it is certain that the architect who worked at Brécy was a great one.

Designed in a period of transition, the garden displays three separate influences. The series of rectangular patterns is typically Renaissance; the sense of proportion and scale

LEFT The rising terraces of Brécy could be the backdrop for an Italian Baroque opera.
BELOW A glimpse of the Norman countryside beyond the iron-work gate at the top of the garden.

A simple box *parterre en
broderie* below the fine
stonework of the first
terrace.

which creates unity and the illusion of continuity (a typical Le Nôtre effect) is Baroque; and the use of fantastical sculpture – mythical birds perched on stone urns, double-headed lions, and so on – is Mannerist.

Monsieur Jacques de Lacretelle of the French Academy, the present owner, and his family have lovingly and carefully restored the house and brought the garden back to life, re-planting the lawns and box edges and creating topiary. The design for the two formal box beds on the lower level was found in a famous eighteenth-century book, *Jardins de Plaisir*, by André Mollet. Orange trees grow in raised white-painted boxes, alternating with agapanthus in terracotta pots. Two small gardens were made in the bays in the façade, separated from the garden by stone balustrades and filled with pink *Hydrangea macrophylla* and fuchsias – a charming, old fashioned combination.

On the second terrace, to either side of a central walk of slightly raised flagstones, two squares divided into four box-edged triangles hold topiary. Under the stone balustrade supporting the curious double-headed lions, a beech hedge hides the retaining wall. A long bed

planted with conical-shaped box, the glossy evergreen Mexican orange *Choisya ternata* grown as a wall shrub beside the steps, and small pale yellow dahlias borders the hedge.

On the third level grassed squares surround two octagonal stone pools and some box topiary. The back border is a mixture of pink and white phlox, white agapanthus, fuchsias, and *Sedum spectabile*. The sides of the two highest terraces are used as cutting gardens full of bright varied dahlias and roses planted with lavender. The back border of the fourth terrace is a gay mixture of pink *Crinum powellii*, hybrid day lilies, yellow sunflowers and hypericum.

Above, on the shallow fifth terrace, the two end walls are decorated with architectural *trompes l'œil*, made of blue-painted wooden trellis-work capped with three stone urns and bordered with stone scrolls and tall yews. Another tiny hidden garden has been planted beyond the gate leading from the house to the original stone bread oven. Despite the charm of the present planting and the evident care given to the garden, the overwhelming impression is one of architectural beauty. Mysterious Brécy is an architect's garden.

FAR LEFT This double-headed lion is one of the many fantastical Mannerist sculptures in the garden.
LEFT A stone urn is another example of the decorative stone work.
BELOW Planting is unobtrusive at Brécy: clipped box, a few shrubs and, as here, pale yellow dahlias set off the architectural strength of the garden.

Manoir de la Bruyère

near Pont-l'Evêque
(Monsieur Hubert Faure)

The narrow lilac walk bordered with hostas and tall white summer hyacinths, *Galtonia candicans*, leads to the twin front doors of the manor house.

LA BRUYERE stands on a hill overlooking the gentle green hills and valleys of Normandy's Pays d'Auge. The view is ravishing: apple orchards, pear trees, distant timbered farms, cottages, grazing cattle and the hedgerows that are typical of this countryside. As soon as the present owner, Monsieur Hubert Faure, took possession of the charming but dilapidated fifteenth-century manor house, he turned his attention to making a garden and landscaping the land. First things first: even before starting the daunting reconstruction of the manor house he invited Russell Page over from England to see the site. The eminent garden designer sensed at once the special qualities of the site, and also its severe limitations. A panorama and a garden seen together distract from each other, he writes in *The Education of a*

The blue garden overlooks a plunging view of green hills and meadows. Pastel pink petunias fill the central ornamental lead container.

Gardener, and here was an immensely attractive panorama which must not be allowed to compete with the garden and win. On a practical level, there were the problems of an extremely windy site and discouragingly stony clay soil.

The master plan was drawn, indicating entrances, paths and the position of new trees. Good earth was brought in to lighten the soil, bulldozers created new levels, an effective drainage system was added, and stone retaining walls and steps were built. Hedges were planted to frame the house and give strong structural lines to the garden, and also to serve as windbreaks. The ground was levelled in front of the manor and then slightly banked to rise away from the house, echoing and continuing the slope of the hillside below. A stone retaining wall was built at a lower level to make a separation for the eye between the manor and the long, lovely, half-timbered cider-press beyond. The ground was also levelled behind the house, facing the view, with stone retaining walls to hold the soil and – equally important – to tell the eye that the house and garden were not about to tumble down the hill. Then, very much as at Hidcote in Gloucestershire, seven garden rooms were planned to surround the house.

The main entrance drive leads to the side of the house, passing between a small pond and the caretaker's thatched cottage before reaching the parking area, well hidden behind large shrubs and hazel trees. From there a wide path of old bricks laid on their sides, bordered by grass and tall shrubs, leads towards an arch in the main yew hedge. The steep pitch of the roof glimpsed through the arch and a view of the cider-press beyond provide the first sight of the architecture that sets the garden in its historical context.

A large rectangular lawn stretches in front of the manor: a green centre, bare except for an old walnut tree, enclosed by thick yew hedges. Buttresses of clipped yew grow out of the hedge at regular intervals, blunting the straight lines and reinforcing the architectural depth of the design. Low clipped box fills the narrow space between the house, the path and the lawn, and is also shaped into geometrical forms, small pyramids and spheres, which grow out of the straight clipped edging. Climbing up the façade – half timbered, and half stone and brick – are the only flowering plants in this central part of the garden: a blue and white *Wisteria sinensis*, and the beautiful white 'Madame Lecoultre' clematis growing through roses – 'Gloire de Dijon', the coral-pink 'François de Jouranville' and the white 'Madame Boucher'.

The central axis of this green garden leads from the double front door (the manor was at one time divided between two families), through the centre of the lawn, past an opening in the hedge, and up a few steps to a narrow closed walk. Here two rows of standard lilacs, all colours, are underplanted with the excellent slug-free *Hosta plantaginea grandiflora*. In August *Galtonia candicans*, giant summer hyacinths, grow through the heart-shaped hosta leaves. A sturdy unpainted wooden seat is placed in front of the beech hedge at the end of the long vista. Behind the hedge, a line of hawthorns backed with maples hides the road beyond. An old wild pear tree grows beyond the hedge to the right of the lilac walk, thickly surrounded by a deep circle of day lilies – an enchanting sight in the Normandy spring.

Beyond the yew hedge a long grass terrace, planted with two orderly lines of twenty-six lime trees, separates the central lawn from the lilac walk. Light and shade seen through these trees give depth and interest to the back part of the garden, adding a sense of mystery.

A flight of stone steps leads down from the end of the house to the corner terrace and to the newest garden, planted between the cider-press and the central lawn's retaining wall. The pink and grey rose garden is laid out on the terrace with an open view of the countryside. Simple geometrical patterns are edged with lavender and silver-leaved plants and filled with a collection of pink roses: 'Grace de Monaco', 'Lady Silvia', 'Madame Meilland', 'Caroline Testout' and some tall 'Queen Elizabeth'. A low stone parapet edged with *Stachys lanata* and pink phlox separates the garden from the view

beyond. A sloping bank, loosely planted with shrub roses, gently divides the garden from the rough hillside below.

Clematis montana tetrarosa and the fine yellow, almost evergreen rose 'Mermaid' grow up the high wall on this side of the manor, and also on the side of the stone steps leading towards the back of the house, and the white and blue gardens. A *Magnolia soulangeana* grows near the back door, charmingly underplanted with small white begonias. A stone pot filled with white campanulas stands at the top of the balustrade.

The garden itself is rectangular in shape, the exact length of the manor it borders. At the centre is the rectangular lawn, its straight borders planted with a profusion of grey-leaved and white-flowering plants: groups of the white hibiscus 'Lady Stanley' and 'Jeanne d'Arc', lavender, artemisias, white phlox, achillea 'The Pearl', and the excellent floribunda rose 'Iceberg' bloom in the summer months, imparting an airy elegance to contrast with the countryside.

Four triangular beds fill the corners of the rectangular garden beyond, each filled with a good selection of summer-flowering plants. Echinops (the metallic blue globe thistle), blue geraniums, hibiscus 'Blue Bird', nepeta, *Aster frikartii* and *Anchusa azurea* alternate with blue petunias and scabious. A decorative lead box planted with pink petunias stands in the middle of the grass, and beyond is the newly planted nuttery. Both these gardens presented a planting problem. As the house is lived in only during the summer, it became a challenge to find interesting white and blue annuals and perennials that flower during July and August.

Four steps at the end of the white garden lead to a lower border edged with pink summer-flowering *Erica cinerea* and planted with a mixture of azaleas, white asters, *Hydrangea grandiflora* and a large group of various ceanothus, which will eventually become a solid bank of blue underlining the blue garden above. Groups of weigela and deutzia grow near the old apple orchard on the slope of the hill, and help to make the transition between the sudden view of the open countryside stretching below and the elegant formality of these two gardens.

ABOVE The small bricked terrace at the top of the *pressoir* is planted in shades of yellow and orange. The flight of stairs leads to a quiet alley of neat lime trees above the green garden.

RIGHT Lilacs edge the retaining wall under the white garden near the old fruit orchard.

Hubert Faure, although pleased with the success of these two lovely gardens, eventually came to feel that the two schemes were perhaps over-fashionable and even a shade tedious with their self-imposed monotony of single colours. Russell Page suggested that the strip of rising ground above the rose garden, which borders the rustic cider-press, could be terraced and planted haphazardly like a *jardin de curé* – the equivalent of the English cottage garden. A mixture of plants and colours would provide a contrast to the orthodox elegance and sobriety of the other gardens.

Now this, the newest creation at La Bruyère, is described by its owner as his miniature Giverny. Bedding-out plants are bought every year (there are no greenhouses or cold frames on the property) and placed in large, arbitrary groups. There is no proper bedding scheme; the form changes every year. The only care taken is in placing the taller plants so as to create height and a feeling of depth. Lupins, echinops, and red and white nicotiana mix with bright zinnias, *Papaver somniferum* (the opium poppy), and large groups of blue asters. Solidago (golden rod) adds touches of yellow, while *Campanula pyramidali* makes lovely high spires of cool blue. There are groups of roses, including pink 'Groutendorf' placed here and there, and clumps of day lilies grow near phlox

and black-eyed rudbeckias. The new garden gives a wonderful impression of summer colour and is exciting and successful when viewed from either above or below. The garden was placed, on purpose, in opposition to the view.

Hubert Faure has become a skilled and dedicated gardener. He began his gardening education by reading widely on the subject, studying catalogues and visiting gardens in France, Britain and America, and now finds design and structure the most important and interesting aspects of gardening. If a planting scheme turns out badly or a crisis is precipitated by the departure of a gardener, the garden will still retain its essential character if

the basic design is sound. Russell Page's original design has stood the test of time, and he continues to provide expert advice. There is a plan to introduce masses of nasturtiums, sunflowers and simple annuals above the cider-press, and a future dream of creating a red garden.

At La Bruyère a synthesis has been achieved within Russell Page's strong structural plan. Principles established at Lawrence Johnston's garden at Hidcote act as the framework for lessons in colour learned at Monet's Giverny, combined with an elegance and restraint inspired by Vita Sackville-West's garden at Sissinghurst. And, as with every real garden, the result is completely individual.

The *jardin de curé* or cottage garden at the side of the cider press is planted purely for colour.

Château de Canon

Mézidon, near Caen
(Monsieur François de Mézerac)

CANON, with its small château, park and fruit gardens, remains just as it was before the French Revolution, unchanged except by time. It was created in the mid-eighteenth century by Jean-Baptiste Elie de Beaumont, a highly successful Parisian barrister with a good private practice, and legal counsellor to a branch of the French royal family. He obtained the Norman property on the fringe of the Pays d'Auge near Caen by marriage, but only after lengthy litigation. During this period of legal delays he travelled to England, the traditional route of the French philosophers, and became a keen observer of the English countryside and of the parks and gardens of the period. With his new friend Horace Walpole, he visited Stowe, where he saw the work of William Kent, and the gardens of the Princess of Wales at Kew. All this would influence and inspire his work on his small estate of 'Canon les Bonnes Gens'.

Why this sudden soubriquet added to the simple name of the property? In 1775, Elie de Beaumont wrote to tell his friend Voltaire of the festival he and his wife had started at Canon, the famous *Fête des Bonnes Gens de Canon*, which yearly attracted hordes of enthusiastic people from all over the surrounding countryside. The day began at nine o'clock in the morning: parades and fanfares, a high mass and a *fête-champêtre*, followed by vespers and fireworks. The purpose of the festivities was the election of the 'Good People' of the region by the Beaumont family and the priests and nobles from the participating villages: the Best Mother, the Best Head of the Family, the Best Son and Daughter and *La Rosière*, or Best Young Maiden. These were the people Elie de Beaumont and his wife were pleased to honour. The large hall used for the ceremonies can still be seen close to the chapel, the stables and outbuildings. The stage has disappeared but the name of *La Salle des Bonnes Gens* remains.

The founding of this yearly tradition came well after Elie de Beaumont finally won legal possession in 1767 of the property on which he worked until his death. A small army of stonemasons, carpenters and sculptors was recruited, and the château was gradually transformed. A storey was added to it, topped by an Italianate roof and stone columns. Stone farm buildings, designed to form two side wings, were also begun. The work was lengthy and costly and continued until Beaumont's death in 1786. 'Canon is a cancer eating away at me', he complained. The architectural work on the

A broken white-painted wooden gate to the side of *Les Chartreuses* opens on to the highly romantic abandoned park.

The view down the six enclosed orchard 'rooms' designed by Voltaire's friend Elie de Beaumont in the eighteenth century. A marble statue of Pomona by Dupaty is framed by leaves and stone.

ABOVE The reverse view
of the flower-filled
chartreuse once ended on a
painted *trompe l'oeil* wall.
ABOVE RIGHT The
Chinese pavilion at
the end of the central axis
of the English-inspired
park was brought from
the demolished Parc des
Ternes in Paris.

buildings and the planning of the park and gardens had become an obsession.

Beaumont's plans for Canon have survived, and bear witness to his deep personal involvement with his small kingdom, as Voltaire called the property. His love of the place consumed his fortune, and his legacy to his son was a mountain of debts. Even his very real grief over the death of his wife became an excuse to beautify Canon. It inspired the neo-classical temple called *La Pleureuse* after the bas-relief on the triangular pediment of a young girl weeping and holding a medallion of Madame de Beaumont. The temple was built at one end of the long central avenue, to balance the Chinese pavilion brought from the Parc des Ternes in Paris after it had been removed to make way for urban expansion.

Geometric alleys and paths were cut through the park, while existing features were converted into follies, or *fabrications*. An old circular dovecote on the axis of the main avenue was cut in two and given a false Roman façade of columns. The tiny ruined Château Bérenger, Canon's first château, built during the reign of Henri IV, was surrounded with an irregular romantic garden: a dark confusion of yews and

laurel trees and small pools. To continue the natural landscaping of the outer park, trees were added, brought from the Duc d'Harcourt's nurseries: Scotch pines, limes and alders, among others. Cascades were added to the river and a stone grotto was built.

Elie de Beaumont, obliged to remain in Paris for his work, had sent to him detailed weekly accounts of the work in progress at Canon. These documents still exist, signed by the various men in charge: Robert Ferey the foreman, Verrier the head gardener, and Eutrope, Canon's steward, bailiff, surgeon and obstetrician.

The lawyer-architect's favourite creation at Canon was the series of orchard and flower gardens he called *Les Chartreuses*, for most of the fruit trees came from the Chartreuse convent near the Luxembourg gardens in Paris. These orchard 'rooms' were built on to the end of the elegant new stone farm buildings. Elie de Beaumont's many letters of instruction to the builder stress the importance of the proportions of the walls, each to be built slightly higher than the next, determined by the height of the arch over each opening in the walls. Six arched openings lead progressively into six of the thirteen gardens. The warm walls sheltered the tender fruit trees: peaches, pears, almonds, figs and occasional grapevines.

Since the nineteenth century, *Les Chartreuses* have become the flower gardens of Canon. The ancient espaliered fruit trees – apples, nectarines, figs, pears and peaches – set against the ivy-covered stone walls now mingle with a glowing display of summer flowers.

The delight of Canon is this walk through the series of flower-filled 'rooms'. The first is planted with deep-rose dahlias, the second with mixed red- and orange-flowering dahlias, bordered with rows of raspberries. Another room is filled with pink and white lavatera and spidery cleomes, and in yet another golden rod, *Solidago canadensis*, and yellow cosmos grow through tall daisies. When you reach the end wall, painted in the eighteenth century as a *trompe l'œil*, turn to watch the play of sunlight through the vines that encircle each opening. The series of doors frames a graceful marble statue by Dupaty of Pomona, the Roman goddess of fruit trees.

This is a garden of effect rather than detail; simple visual delights combine architecture, colour and great charm. Set behind the rusted iron gates in the side of *Les Chartreuses*, the park, with its eighteenth-century trees, follies and statues, offers the pleasure of nostalgia. Its formal, classical aspect is represented still by the large reflecting pool behind the château. Old trees – some no doubt planted by Elie de Beaumont himself, others added over a hundred years ago – surround it. Marble busts on decorative pedestals are reflected in the still water. Of the original thirty-two Italian copies of antique models of goddesses and actors, twenty-five remain throughout the park. They keep alive the time-dimmed memory of Elie de Beaumont's *petit royaume*.

Even though Beaumont's legacy was the mountain of debts which forced his son to sell even the furniture from the château, Canon les Bonnes Gens remains. It has survived revolution, occupations, bombardments, tempests and the ever-rising costs of maintenance. Courageously, Elie de Beaumont's descendants have kept his memory alive by maintaining Canon. Members of the family come down at weekends and holidays to help with the work. Gardeners and servants have, like the Good People, disappeared, but Canon continues.

One of the twenty-five marble busts placed around the large cloudy reflecting pool behind the château. These are seventeenth-century Italian copies of Roman sculpture.

Château du Pontrancart

near Dieppe
(Monsieur et Madame Bemberg)

PONTRANCART appears to have been used as a family seat since its origin, although not all of the documents concerning its history have survived. The château was first mentioned in the middle of the fourteenth century, when it belonged to the Coquereaumonts, one of the most powerful Norman families, whose most illustrious member was allied by marriage to the English royal family. His influence and lands stretched as far as Picardy, yet he chose to make Pontrancart his favourite seat. The direct line of the Coquereaumont family died out a few generations later, and the property changed hands several times before it was bought in the early seventeenth century by Monsieur de Lontot, a ship-builder from Dieppe. He built a large house in pink brick. The façade, overlooking the south-east ter-

OPPOSITE *Sedum spectabilis* backed by cosmos in the pink garden 'room'.
BELOW Borders of golden rudbeckia, marigolds and antirrhinums in this garden of annuals.

race, probably covers the earlier foundations.

The château was modified during the second half of the eighteenth century: while the austere north façade, in the style of Louis XIII, was left intact, the south façade was decorated with white pilasters. A 1765 plan of the property shows vast *parterres à la française* on the site of the present-day water garden, beyond the bend in the river that encircles the château and its out-buildings. (These, apart from the sixteenth-century water-mill at the entrance to the property, are all contemporary with the château.)

Monsieur Bemberg, the father of the present owner, bought the property in 1930 and set out to restore it to its former glory as a family home and a place of leisure. An English lady, Miss K. Lloyd Jones, helped to design a geometrical garden, which blends perfectly with the sober formality of the château. A kitchen garden was laid out on the far side of the moat, with each vegetable grown in its own separate compart-

A silver tapestry on the terrace overlooking the flower garden.

ment, edged traditionally with yew. This garden was abandoned during the Second World War, and the untended yews grew huge and wild; after the war it was decided to maintain their size but to shape them into strong neat hedges. The informality of an English garden could be hidden behind these high, thick hedges beyond the flowered banks of the moat.

Pontrancart is a summer garden, planned for the briefest of seasons. Gardens are rarely designed for one short flowering — except perhaps at Balmoral where the gardens are brought to perfection for the yearly month-long visit of the royal family. Monsieur and Madame Bemberg traditionally spend half of August and all of September at Pontrancart and a garden in full flower welcomes them. Throughout the rest of the year, the garden is bare, except for the decorative parterre set in the grassed terrace in front of the château.

It was only after long hesitation that the Bembergs replaced the traditional gravel border around the château with a lawn and four parterres of silver-leaved plants: lavender, thyme and santolina, mixed with box, all clipped low to prevent flowering and encourage thickness. The parterres are framed by bricks laid horizontally, and the four corners are marked by thick vertical conifers, planted to give stability to the flat silver design.

The moat marks the transition from the formal *parterres à la française* in front of the house to the natural landscape beyond, a mixture of soft, undulating grassy hills, distant woods and a line of poplar trees on the far side of the river. The water-mill near the entrance gate and a herd of cows in the lush meadow behind the kitchen garden create an idealized rural scene around the château and out-buildings. Peace and well-being reign.

Monsieur Bemberg has asked Russell Page to design a water garden on the meadow, and now a series of small canals has been dug and many aquatic and water-loving plants have been planted, but the garden is not yet mature. It will take some years of growth before this new venture blends into the surrounding countryside.

To the right of the moat a long border, backed by the main hedge of the kitchen garden, dazzles the eye. A mass of large,

Volume and height used to good effect in the white garden 'room', in front of a long grey roof.

spectacular clumps of bright colour, visible from the château and terrace, is the overture to a group of gardens behind the yew hedges. These consist of connecting 'rooms', each planted with annuals in a single colour range. The harmonious colour effect, progressing from room to room, is so lovely that it is easy to forget that it is composed largely of simple cottage plants: cosmos, marigolds, lavatera, ageratum and zinnias. Perennials, mainly phlox and delphiniums, an essential part of all summer borders, make up barely ten per cent of the borders. Even the perennials are treated as annuals, and are suppressed wherever a stronger variety or a better colour is available.

Monsieur Bemberg is very interested in the new American varieties of late summer-flowering hemerocallis and orders them every year from the United States. These new day lilies are tried out on a testing ground before being planted out either in the spot in the border best suited to their flowering colour, or in the new water garden.

Most of the garden 'rooms' are planted with a variety of annuals all flowering in the same colour range: for example, zinnias, antirrhinums, coreopsis and rudbeckia make up the

golden garden; other 'rooms' are planted exclusively with all the pink, red and raspberry shades available in antirrhinums. They provide an excellent lesson in how best to use the many heights and shades of one plant species in a garden.

The delight of the garden, and its main point of interest, is the perfectly synchronized flowering of a large variety of plants, truly a *tour de force*. Normal flowering periods are either delayed or advanced by carefully calculated sowing times and bedding out. Antoni Aleix, the head gardener, is responsible for the planning of this yearly miracle, although Monsieur and Madame Bemberg decide the colour scheme.

Flowering is prolonged by intensive dead-heading, and watering is also an essential part of the general maintenance: the rotary sprinklers are turned on each evening for several hours. The plants are staked with pea-sticks to avoid their being flattened by the Normandy rain and the action of the sprinkler. Maintenance is meticulous, but concentrated within a brief period, whereas the work in other gardens is year-long. Could the six-week garden at Pontrancart be the formula for the ideal holiday garden?

Le Vasterival

Sainte Marguerite, near Dieppe
(La Princesse Sturdza)

LE VASTERIVAL is much more than a garden, and yet very different from a conventional park. This spectacularly hilly land watered by natural springs might better be described as 'a botanical landscape for all seasons'. The Princesse Sturdza began planting at Le Vasterival in 1957. The site, swept by strong sea winds, was thick with brambles and disfigured by rotting tree stumps and dense overgrown thickets. She has slowly and patiently cleaned, reclaimed and planted the land to reveal its full potential.

Any description of Le Vasterival must begin with a mention of the gardener and her unique methods of gardening and landscaping. Greta Sturdza has a true vocation for gardening, a strong commitment, and a need to instruct others in her acquired techniques. Nothing is left to chance in the realization of her work. That the plants at Le Vasterival grow luxu-

The park seen through the branches of a *Magnolia cylindrica* in flower.

riantly, that their flowering season is longer here than elsewhere, is due neither to the humid Norman climate, nor to any special quality in the soil, and certainly not to specific treatments or fertilizers for the plants. The Princess's unequivocal success is due to the close attention that she pays to the planting, pruning and aftercare of every plant, shrub and tree. There is no secret; there is method. Greta Sturdza's motto is her dogma: 'work for the plant, work ten times over to plant'. The superb condition of her plants is the result of the meticulous preparation that precedes every planting.

As you walk along the shady walks and over the open hilly land of Le Vasterival, you are struck by the absence of the architectural follies and artifices that traditionally embellish most parks and gardens. In other gardens, climbers are trained to twine and fall through pergolas; here, trees are their sole support. The natural shade cast by trees over the many paths and walks replaces the formal clipped green tunnels found elsewhere. Every tree's natural habit of growth is respected: there are no curious

geometrical shapes, and the trees are pruned only to improve their condition. There are no enclosed spaces between clipped hedges, and the landscape flows naturally; view follows view at every curve in the paths. Nature is aided but, above all, respected – even the bridges over the numerous streams and rills throughout the property are only simple wooden planks placed wherever a crossing is needed.

Greta Sturdza's first concern in 1957, when she took possession of the property, was to protect future planting from the force of the dominant winds. Perched on the heights of Ste Marguerite near Dieppe, Le Vasterival is exposed to the full strength of all the winds off the Channel, and so conifers, oaks, rhododendrons, holly and laurels were planted as permanent windbreaks. The Princess also uses less permanent windbreaks – a series of movable folding screens of perforated black plastic sheeting – to protect recent plantings. The winter of 1978 will always be remembered for the terrible storm that ravaged the Normandy coast and felled over a hundred trees at Le

Vasterival alone. It was an enormous and heartbreaking job to remove the stumps and once more clear the land. New trees were planted to replace those lost, and eventually to create new views, but the character of the landscape is already altered. The removal of one of the older trees that sheltered a fine group of shade-loving large-leaved rhododendrons, hellebores and camellias, has already turned a shady corner into open sunny land, now replanted with a suitable collection of sun-lovers: cistus, helianthemum, phormium and others. The choice of plants is always guided by a careful analysis of the soil and the position of the site, as well as by the colours and tones of the surrounding flowers and foliage.

Trees play a major role at Le Vasterival – evergreens and deciduous trees, flowering trees and trees with decorative bark, like the two lovely birches *Betula nigra* and *Betula papyrifera*. Certain trees merit special mention, particularly those that give a wonderful show of autumn colour: *Viburnum opulus*, the guelder rose, covered in winter with red translucent fruit; *Viburnum opulus* 'Sterile', the 'snowball' tree,

and *V. opulus* 'Alnifolium' with large veined leaves. Maples include *Acer campestre* 'Nanum', shaded gold to red, and the orange *Acer palmatum* 'Cherry Ingram'; other autumn foliage trees include prunus, hamamelis, the feathery-leaved *Cotinus coggygria*, *Photinia villosa*, covered with bright red fruits, *Nyssa sylvatica*, the rare *Nyssa sinensis* and *Cornus florida rubra*.

The soil has an average reading of 5 on the pH scale, perfect for growing rhododendrons and azaleas. The high ground at Le Vasterival was chosen as the best site for a massive planting of them, together with huge clumps of blue-flowering hortensias – one of the great glories of the garden. The giant flower-heads are left on the hortensias until spring, as the dried heads, in shades of bronze, mauve and metallic-grey, make a very attractive autumn and winter display.

A clump of *Cortaderia selloana*, the evergreen perennial pampas grass from Argentina, grown high through a group of hortensias, gives an unexpected and interesting combination of plants, their silvery plumes making a fine effect against the darker background.

ABOVE CENTRE Borders of massed hortensias are one of the glories of Le Vasterival.
ABOVE Cyclamens are amongst the many ground-cover plants used in the park. Notice the planted 'islands' in the grass.

Colour fills Le Vasterival in spring. In places the ground is carpeted with a huge variety of primroses, brilliant botanical tulips and special hellebores, grown and selected by Greta Sturdza. Each dazzling white flower has a perfect shape and stands well above the leaves of the plant. The earliest bulbs begin to bloom in February, at the same time as the first rhododendrons come into flower: *Rhododendron* 'Christmas Cheer', R. *roblianum* and R. *præcox*, mixed with their botanical cousins the pieris, whose brilliant red young shoots make it one of the most beautiful shrubs for gardens or woodland. In summer, the woods are a mass of arborescent heathers and stiff-spiked flowering digitalis.

Anyone with an experienced eye can see that

every square inch of land at Le Vasterival has been put to good use. The brooks and all the spring water drain into the valley which has become, logically, a home for moisture-loving plants. There is a spectacular planting of large groups of blue, mauve and white *Iris kæmpferi*, among the rodgersia, senecios and a jungle of giant gunnera. Further on, a mixed planting of agapanthus 'Headbourne' and pink and white flowering astilbes covers a bank, and candelabra primulas grow in clusters along the water's edge. In spring, their twenty-four-inch flowering stalks form dense tiers on the western banks.

A narrow grassy path leads up the hill towards another landscape: first, there is a group of well-placed statuesque conifers, underplanted with summer- and winter-flowering heathers, and beyond this miniature forest are clumps of strongly scented hamamelis. The spider-like yellow and reddish flowers perfume the walk. Another scent typical of this garden is that of *Cercidiphyllum japonicum*, a small rare Japanese tree that turns a smoky-pink and yellow in autumn. Pink, mauve, yellow and ivory-white flowering heathers shade the slopes, making a patchwork of colour throughout the year. Large beds, each with its own dominant colour, decorate the bottom of the valley: one for example, is a mixture of yellow roses, golden variegated ivies and *Kerria japonica*, with its alternating leaves and buttercup yellow flowers. It is impossible to describe here each planting composition, but interesting to understand the technique behind their creation.

All the beds are cut out of an uninterrupted stretch of grass: an 'island' is made and prepared for each new project. Then the bed is filled with the appropriate soil for the selected plants. One bed may hold just one subject, a tree or shrub, while a neighbouring plot, a few feet away, may contain two or three plants. There is nothing arbitrary in this planting; it is the Princess's provisional first stage of design. Later, she joins one plot to another and, finally, the whole becomes a long curving border of integrated plants.

The common denominator at Le Vasterival is the use of ground-cover plants throughout the property: on open ground, in the wood-

Winter-flowering witch hazel.

lands and in the bog garden. They are the essential element in every design, and no garden in France has a larger selection of them. Their rich variety constitutes the decorative element that unites every composition of trees and shrubs. Pachysandra with the azaleas, *Cornus canadensis* between the rhododendrons, ivies or variegated vincas around the roses and *Kerria japonica*, and acæna, lamium and ajuga to provide colour in the woods throughout the year. The definition of ground cover has a special significance at Le Vasterival: many plants massed together are used for this purpose: primulas, hellebores, tiarella and the pure-white-flowering *Kardamine trifoliata* in the shade. Mulch is the other essential ground cover: Greta Sturdza mulches all the beds and various planting groups lavishly with two inches of leaf-mould, the prime component in the nourishing blanket that keeps the soil cool and moist in summer and protects against frost in the winter. It also discourages weeds throughout the year.

The logical end to a visit to Le Vasterival is the plateau, the only completely flat part of this hilly property. Screened by a grove of trees behind the main house, the plateau has a series of large traditional borders filled with all the classic perennials: phlox, delphiniums, lupins and lysimachia, mixed with roses. Certain roses, including 'Queen Elizabeth', grow as high as small trees, and heavily scented old-fashioned roses, often mingled with clematis, scramble into the old apple trees. 'Oliver Vibert', 'Dr Van Fleet', 'Albertine' and 'Kathleen Harrop' bloom softly among the branches. When weather permits, Greta Sturdza has tea in this part of the garden with her pupils: friends and botanists from all over Europe join the popular classes she gives at different times of the year.

Greta Sturdza, like her predecessor Gertrude Jekyll at the turn of the century in England, has introduced, developed and put into practice many gardening techniques at Le Vasterival. And, like Gertrude Jekyll, she is a true innovator, with a fine instinct for harmony in plant association.

Parc Floral des Moutiers

Varengeville, near Dieppe
(Famille Mallet)

WHEN GUILLAUME MALLET bought Les Moutiers in 1898, he was probably struck by the superb view from the wild, humid and impenetrable site, overlooking a wide bay of white-capped waves. As a gardener, the factor most important to him was the nature of the soil of his future domain; a soil highly favourable for the cultivation of rhododendrons and azaleas.

Long before, young Guillaume Mallet had unknowingly begun preparing himself indirectly for the work that would fill his life: he was passionately interested in painting, the decorative arts and music; he had already begun to collect old fabrics, ceramics and paintings, his family delighted in the art of tapestry-making and fine embroidery, and he went on botanical trips with his mother through Italy and England. When his military career ended prematurely, the stage was set for the adventure of Les Moutiers.

First Lutyens, the brilliant English architect, was chosen to design and build the house. Then Guillaume Mallet embarked on the ambitious project which would fill his life for forty years: the laying out of a large botanical park. He adopted the ideas of Shaftesbury, who had inspired William Kent, the great landscape architect of the eighteenth century. His other masters were his favourite painters, Claude Lorrain and Gaspard Dughet, and his bible was a collection of drawings signed Claude Gellée (Claude Lorrain). Every vista in the park would be inspired by a drawing: he reshaped the existing terrain, hollowing out paths, planting many-branched trees and establishing groves, carefully taking into account levels of light and shade. The evergreen hollies and oaks that formed the background for the three-dimensional paintings he created in the park have now reached full maturity.

The choice of colours was the result of patient work. To minimize mistakes, Mallet used pieces of eighteenth-century velvet and damask as colour references for his choice of plants, concentrating particularly on the hundreds of rhododendron species and hybrids grown in the nursery. June is the time to enjoy his composition of rich, glowing Renaissance blues and reds resulting from the mixture of silvery-blue *Cedrus atlantica* 'Glauca' with the red-flowering rhododendrons 'Alarm', 'Devil de Carnot' and 'Ascot Brilliant'.

A plan dated 1904 bears witness to Lutyens' collaboration with Gertrude Jekyll in laying out the garden. Gertrude Jekyll's approach was expressed in the articles she wrote regularly for *Country Life*, all carefully cut out and kept for reference by M. Mallet. Seen from the road, the beautiful borders on both sides of the main entrance drive were directly inspired by her advice on planting compositions: yuccas, anemones, roses and delphiniums were planted amongst the perennials and massed annual heliotropes. Even today Miss Jekyll's rules of composition are faithfully followed, although problems of maintenance have banished the annuals and slightly modified the original plan.

A tapestry effect is achieved by mixing *Rosa rugosa* 'Blanc Double de Coubert' and 'Roseraie de l'Hay' in front of the border with *Deutzia gracilis* and the pale blue *Iris germanica*. The spectacular tree peonies 'Rock's variety' make a focal point in the border, and phlox, anemones and aconites are used near a variety of shrub roses: the lovely hybrid musk 'Cornelia', 'Erfurt', 'Sparrieshoop', 'Felicia' and 'Frau Karl Druschki'. The border is edged

with hebe 'Pagei', an excellent ground-cover plant, *Stachys lanata*, *Saxifraga moschata* and *sarmentosa*, geranium 'Buxton Blue', *Liatris spicata*, hosta and *Anaphalis triplinervis*. In the round courtyard, originally planted with four cypresses where now only two survive, a mat-forming rosemary is a strong element in the planting scheme, as well as *Lamium* 'Beacon Silver', *Rosa* 'Yesterday', thyme, *Daphne tangutica*, *Potentilla* 'Manchu', *Rhododendron williamsianum* and heuchera. *Spiræa thunbergii* grows next to a white-flowering camellia and the abelias 'Edward Goucher' *grandiflora* and *englerana*, *Asperula odorata* and saxifrage. Old-fashioned

OPPOSITE Mixed borders lead to the Lutyens house. ABOVE An *Azalea palestrina* in full flower.

The rose-covered brick pergola is bordered with iris, ferns, aquilegia and caryopteris.

roses still cover the walls: 'Lady Hillingdon' and 'La Follette' were brought back to Varengeville from the south of France, where Guillaume Mallet used to spend the months of January and February in a Lutyens-designed villa at Ranguin, near Grasse.

Hebe salicifolia 'Spendler's seedling', *Cimicifuga dahurica* and white Spanish lilacs create a fountain effect against the long dark side wall planted with yews on one side of the garden. This is a white garden: 'Iceberg' roses and white lily-blooming tulips fill the nine square openings in the paving stones. A box border encloses *Anaphalis triplinervis*. *Hosta sieboldiana* 'Elegans' and *H. plantaginea* 'Grandiflora' and wall-grown *Hydrangea petiolaris* and *Viburnum semperflorens nanum* fill the shady corners.

The old rose garden, laid out concentrically around a sundial, was completely redesigned. The once closed area now opens on to an orchard of *Magnolia* × *læbneri* 'Moutiers', a fragrant white wood in April. To accommodate visitors, the rose beds have been moved to the four corners of the garden, enhancing Lutyens' plan in the Gertrude Jekyll style. A cypress backs each of the four 'grey' corners planted with rosemary, 'Hidcote' lavender, 'Dutch' lavender, senecio, *Linum narbonense* and the blue-leafed *Mahonia trifoliata glauca*. The excellent recurrent rose, 'Golden Wings' adds a touch of light to the garden, and aquilegias and brown irises make a lovely June

design at the foot of a pergola, while *Ceanothus impressus* makes a blue background punctuated by four clipped balls of *Viburnum tinus* '*purpurea*'. Blue and white agapanthus are planted at the foot of the wall, near *Veronica spicata*, white crinum, dark blue tradescantia, pale blue *Viola cornuta* and low blue campanulas.

A number of ground-cover plants shelter under the pergola: *Saxifraga fortunei*, *rubrifolia* and the autumn-flowering 'Wada's pink'. Planted among spiraeas and ferns are a mixture of astrantia and *Geranium majenta*, variety 'Russell Prichart'. Old-fashioned roses clamber over the pergola: 'Cécile Brunner', 'Alister Stella Gray', 'Albéric Barbier' and 'Leverkusen'.

The pergola cuts across the axis of the entrance alley at right angles to the round courtyard, where *Rosa* 'Wedding Day' climbs across a white wall and into the cypress. The perspective from it culminates in a Chinese pavilion, which joins two of the most architectural parts of the garden: the paved garden and the rose garden.

The Chinese pavilion shelters a copy of Donatello's statue of David and Goliath, and has slender pillars of the local Varengeville brick, which in summer are wreathed in the pale orange-flowering eglantine rose 'Mrs Oakly Fish'. An enormous *Magnolia grandiflora* 'Treyviensis' is carefully pruned each year for wind resistance and to keep its shape proportionate to the size of the pavilion. A few feet from the pavilion, a brick path leads through shade into full light towards a spectacular border, fully seventy yards long and six feet wide, planted with *Hydrangea paniculata* 'Grandiflora' evenly balanced with the hybrid musk rose 'Penelope' and *Polygonum campanulatum*, and enhanced by the progressive flowering of clematis 'Mme E. André', 'Ville de Lyon' and 'Royal Velours'. Two varieties of wisteria are grown as standards, *Wisteria venusta* and *W. sinensis* 'Alba'. Creamy rose-flowering chrysanthemums prolong the colour scheme into autumn. The border marks the starting point for a variety of interesting shrubs: stranvaesia 'Redstart', the hardy mound-forming *Ceanothus thyrsiflorus repens* and a tall *Fagus sylvatica* 'Dawyck', the Norman cypress whose russet autumnal foliage lasts until February. The pervasive influence of Gertrude Jekyll is particularly striking in the summer-flowering park.

Part of the upper garden, called the Pasture, was an ideal spot for mixed groups of flowering shrubs, their various colours and textures dictating the elegant layout. The best time to visit this garden is April, when the bell-shaped flowers of rhododendrons 'Temple Bells', 'Bow Bells' and 'Rosy Bells' stand out against a background of fragrant tree heaths, *Erica arborea* 'Alpina'. The blue-flowering rhododendrons 'Sapphire', 'Blue Diamond' and 'Blue Tit' form another tableau near the lovely pale lemon-flowering Exbury hybrid rhododendron 'Carita'. Elsewhere a group of amber-pink-flowering rhododendron 'Alison Johnstone' shines through the massed blue tones of *Rhododendron augustinii*, *R. russatum* over a planting of dwarf rhododendrons. During the same season, the park is filled with magnolias in flower: *Magnolia denudata*, *M. læbneri* and *M. stellata*, as well as the magnificent hybrid and Japanese camellias. *Pieris japonica* grow throughout the park, their large panicles of fragrant bell-shaped flowers a soft touch of light in the landscape.

When Charles de Noailles was a young man of eighteen, he brought some rhododendron seeds to Les Moutiers, a present from Lawrence Johnston, the great gardener and creator of Hidcote in Gloucestershire and Les Serres de la Madonne in the south of France, who was convinced that rhododendrons would

thrive at Varengeville. Two of the varieties grown from seeds were greenish-white and white flushed rose in colour. Monsieur Halope of Cherbourg crossed the two shrubs with the American 'Rose Bay', *Rhododendron maximum*, and obtained the remarkable May-flowering *Rhododendron halopeanum* which grows abundantly at Les Moutiers, near *Rhododendron griffithianum*. Tall white-flowering broom makes a

luminous foreground for the brilliant copper-red young growths of *Photinia* 'Robusta' and *P. glabra* 'Rubens', a sealing-wax red that harmonizes with the blood-red shoots of Japanese maples. Late-flowering rhododendrons with blotched flowers bloom gloriously throughout May and June. These old species deserve a new popularity: they are frost-resistant and provide a range of warm colours rarely available for parks and large gardens.

A path named after Mary Mallet, who has dedicated herself totally to her father-in-law's work, is planted with white-flowering shrubs, including the hardy and floriferous *Rhododendron yunnanense* and *Azalea* 'Palestrina'. In sum-

mer this part of the garden becomes a tapestry of shades of pink, orange and white. Deep in the park *Eucryphias × intermedia*, 'Nymansay', *cordifolia* and *lucida* grow in tall columns, perfuming the air with abundant, butterfly-like flowers. The large, fragrant, pure white rhododendron 'Polar Bear' is a lovely sight in summer.

In the depths of the park there are many natural springs which were diverted to meander their way through the heart of the woods, thickly planted with *Iris kæmpferi*. Reflected in the water, the delicate pale blue, deep mauve, violet and white of the irises give the effect of an Impressionist painting. Further on, a valley

ABOVE and OPPOSITE The glowing colours of rhododendrons and hydrangeas are set off by a background of conifers and evergreens.

was planted with late-blooming astilbes to make another tableau which, following the late June-flowering azaleas in the dales, is characteristic of the landscaping of the park. The Ghent hybrid azaleas with their honeysuckle-like flowers grow in the vale of Ghent, while the tall American hybrid *Azalea occidentalis* thrives in the vale of La Source, near a river of ferns *Matteucia struthiopteris*.

Among the many breathtaking visual effects at Les Moutiers is the mass of glowing red June-flowering rhododendrons framed by blue cedars at the back of the park. The June-flowering rhododendrons are generally richer in colour than the white and pink May varieties, the exception being the Mollis azaleas that can turn a hillside into a sheet of flame in May. The shades here range from pale yellow to deeper tones of ochre to soft orange and deepest red. Gertrude Jekyll planned the colour scheme and Guillaume Mallet completed the composition by planting the contrasting background of blue cedars. The flaming colours of the flowering azaleas are set in high relief by the cold blue of the conifers.

In summer, the park overflows with masses of hydrangeas: the large *Hydrangea paniculata* 'Grandiflora' shelters against a group of *Cryptomeria japonica* 'Elegans', and throughout the grounds huge white, pink and blue bouquets of flowering hydrangeas bloom next to aralias and the highly fragrant *Clethra alnifolia*, the 'sweet pepper bush'. In autumn, the park is ablaze with an infinite variety of changing foliage, set off by the background of blue cedars, evergreen oaks and holly. Maples, oaks, parrotia and nyssa rival each other in brilliance. The bright holly berries and the fruits of the mountain ash and the skimmias are a presage of winter, a rewarding season at Les Moutiers thanks to the abundance of fine conifers and the striking view of the sea. Occasionally the landscape is covered with a fine carpet of snow.

The association of Gertrude Jekyll and Guillaume Mallet, followed by the faithful continuation of their work by Mary Mallet and her son Robert, fully justify the park and gardens' classification in 1980 as a historic monument, protected by the state. The house, one of Lutyens' masterpieces, was classified in 1975.

Claude Monet's Garden

*Giverny, near Vernon
(Institut de France)*

GIVERNY is a painter's garden, created by the father of Impressionism, whose dedication was such that he often said that nothing in the world interested him but his painting and his flowers. All the themes that were to obsess Monet until his death at Giverny in 1926 were visible in the garden: flowers massed in groups of solid colours, water to reflect the changing sky, and the water-lilies which inspired his great series of paintings, *Les Décorations des Nymphéas*.

Monet's discovery of a place to live in the quiet valley of the Epte marked a turning point in his life, at a time when he was beset by financial worries and critical failure and was grieving the death of his first wife. The small village of Giverny lies spread out along the low hills facing the valley of the Seine, where two streams, the tiny Ru and the Epte, divide the Ile-de-France from the province of Normandy. Monet became increasingly attached to this '*si beau pays*', 'this beautiful land', and it was a perfect home for a painter fascinated by light and water: 'The subject is of secondary importance to me: what I want to reproduce is what exists between the subject and me'. The ever-changing soft light of the river valley was the real subject, and Giverny was the place to capture it.

Monet was fifty years old in 1890 when he managed to borrow enough money – almost ruining Durand-Ruel his dealer in the process – to buy Le Pressoir, the house he had already lived in for seven years. The long rough pink house with an exotic air had belonged to a merchant from Guadeloupe. The property covered two and a half acres sloping down to the Chemin du Roy, the road at the end of the village. A small local railway ran along the edge

of the road at the foot of the walled orchard. The garden as it existed was heavily planted with dark yews and overgrown box trees, and was depressingly bourgeois. Monet, who hated all formality, at once removed the box, and only allowed the two yews in front of the house to remain as a concession to his second wife, Alice. The plan of the garden remained geometrical, with a broad central avenue leading straight from the house to the front gate set in the bottom wall. Nasturtiums climbed up the archways and spilled on to the gravel paths. Several smaller parallel paths lined either side of the garden – with rectangular beds to the left of the house below the barn, and a series of square beds to the right of the central avenue. But the straight lines were soon to disappear under Monet's lavish planting.

The year after buying Le Pressoir, Monet wrote to the poet Mallarmé, 'I have much to do, a quantity of new paintings to finish. And moreover, I must confess, I leave Giverny with difficulty, above all now that I'm fixing up the house and the garden to my taste'. Monet was busy erecting a light metal framework over the wooden balcony in front of the house and raising metal archways over the central avenue. He had all the metal-work throughout the garden painted a bright leaf green, the same Impressionist colour he used for the doors and shutters on the outside of the house, to harmonize with the greens of the garden.

Monet worked alone in the garden, except when helped by his children. His days were long, starting at five o'clock every morning, when he walked through the garden, obsessively inspecting and dead-heading the plants in the early light before taking his canvases and paints over to the left bank of the

RIGHT Monet's *Nymphéas et Agapanthes.*
OPPOSITE White wisteria on the Japanese bridge behind a young Judas tree in May.
BELOW A massed underplanting of white and pink *Impatiens sultanii.*

Epte, where he was painting a series of studies of light on the poplar trees. By 1892 improved finances and a further loan from Durand-Ruel enabled him to hire a head gardener, Félix Breuil, who was recommended to him by his friend Octave Mirbeau, the writer and art critic. Soon M. Breuil was joined by five under-gardeners. Three greenhouses were built below the barn used by Monet as his studio, and were a source of great delight to him, for he continued to collect plants throughout his life; but they were also a cause of anxiety, as when both he and his wife spent a cold winter's night assuring themselves that the new heating system was working properly. The old orchard was abandoned, and instead Monet planted Japanese flowering cherries and apple trees on the lawn near a path bordered with his favourite bearded iris and oriental poppies. Clematis were grown on high metal supports, and roses covered the central arches over the nasturtium-

bordered central avenue. Monochromatic groups of strong-coloured flowers were planted throughout the garden, alternating with beds of paler flowers. Details were unimportant – massed colour and texture dominated the garden. Every season brought new colour and new compositions: golden daffodils were followed by bright red tulips underplanted with forget-me-nots; lilacs, wisteria and irises brought mauve and purple into the garden. In June the lilies, delphiniums, peonies, lupins and Canterbury bells came into flower and massed asters, glowing dahlias, sunflowers and graceful Japanese anemones filled the garden from September until the first frosts. Roses flowered everywhere: dazzling swatches of colour hung over the central walk, standard bushes dominated the beds and climbers wreathed special metal supports, throwing colour into the air. Monet's only prejudice was against plants with variegated leaves – colours must remain solid and true.

On Tuesday, 1 February 1883, Monet went to Paris to see an exhibition of Japanese prints at the Durand-Ruel gallery. He had already been collecting them for over ten years, having discovered his first prints wrapped around objects he bought in Amsterdam during a trip to Holland, and had long been influential in spreading the Japanese influence among his contemporaries. By chance he met his friend Pissarro at the Durand-Ruel exhibition, but while Pissarro was carried away by the economy and strength of line in the exhibits, Monet was fascinated by the images of exotic plants, still water and Japanese bridges. Coincidentally, four days later he signed the final papers giving him ownership of the strip of land on the other side of the railway, bought to make a second garden, the Japanese water garden.

Time was lost getting permission to make changes in the terrain. Whilst at Rouen painting the Cathedral series, Monet was forced to write to the Prefect of the Eure to ask permission to renew the water in the pools to be dug. 'In view of the cultivation of aquatic plants, I would like to install a *prise d'eau* in the Epte. I plan to build two small bridges in light wood over the stream'. In mid-July he sent a second letter to the Prefect, justifying his project in some detail,

> . . . I want you to know that the aforementioned 'culture of water plants' is less ambitious than the phrase implies, as it concerns only an object of amusement to please the eye, and also to provide inspiration for my painting; in fact I will grow only plants such as water-lilies, reeds and various irises in the pool, plants that grow naturally along our river, and there is no question of polluting the water.

Monet was still at Rouen when the local stalemate ended and permission was given to begin work. Overjoyed, he rushed to see the director of the Jardin des Plantes at Rouen, and was offered coveted plants from the municipal greenhouses and precious advice on how to establish them at Giverny. He also made time to visit all the local nurseries and sent home baskets of plants.

The latter part of the year was occupied in preparing the new garden and building the two bridges. The larger curved Japanese bridge over the pool first appeared in a painting finished in the winter of 1895, before Monet left for a two-month trip to Norway. Worried by the news of a cold spell seizing the countryside around Giverny, Monet wrote a concerned and touching letter home: '. . . I imagine the skater's joy, but I tremble for the garden. Are you sure the pool is free of ice? It would be too sad if all the plants perished . . .' A second letter to his wife rapidly followed: '. . . I am appalled by the news about my poor roses, and await more disasters. Have you thought about covering the Japanese peonies, at the very least it would amount to murder if you have not already done so'. Every gardener will recognize Monet's anguish. The Japanese peonies were special treasures, some a present from Japanese friends, others ordered directly from Japan to grow around the pool in the new water garden. From this period on, Monet sold paintings primarily in order to pay the increasing cost of the garden and allow himself the luxury of buying new plants.

Monet's close friend Gustave Geffroy described the new garden in his book *Claude Monet, sa vie, son temps, son œuvre*, published in Paris in 1922:

Monet designed the garden and laid out the plants, the willows unfurling their green tresses, the bamboo springing forth, the massed rhododendrons bordering the paths; and he sowed the pond with water-lilies, whose free roots float in the waters, spread with large pads bursting forth with white, rose, mauve and green flowers. Monet comes to stand on the wisteria-covered Japanese bridge and judge the painting he created.

The originality of the water garden was that it was laid out like a painting; the sky seems present only in the water, the changing reflections deepening the colours or lightening the surface of Monet's mirror.

Two years later, Georges Truffaut described the completed garden in an article written for the review *Jardinage*.

The pool, fed by the waters of the river Epte, is surrounded by golden-branched weeping willows. The ground and the banks are massed with plants such as heather, ferns, laurel, rhododendrons, azaleas and holly. The water's edges are shaded on one side by abundant shrub roses. On the other side a large clump of bamboo forms a thick wood. Every known variety of water-lily grows in the pool. On the banks, irises intermingle with tree peonies, groups of cytisus and Judas trees. The banks are also covered with large-leaved winter heliotrope on clipped lawns of thalictrum, various ferns with pale, downy, pink or white flowers and wisteria. There are also tamarisks and the whole garden is filled with standard and shrub roses.

Cézanne passed through Giverny in November 1894, before the water garden showed its full promise. He visited the front garden, the Clos Normand, and saw Monet's latest paintings. A man of few words, he observed, 'Monet is but an eye ... but, good God, what an eye!' Monet increasingly used the pool as an extension to his failing eyesight. He continued to paint details in the water garden – a group of day-lilies, irises, the branches of the weeping willows touching the water – but his dominant obsession remained

the juxtaposition of the sky reflected in water and the water-lilies. On 11 August 1908, he wrote to Gustave Geffroy: 'These landscapes of water and reflected light have become an obsession. It's beyond my old man's strength; nevertheless I want to express what I feel'.

Monet's life became progressively sadder and more difficult. His wife died in May 1911. His dear daughter-in-law Blanche remained with him, but the death of her husband, Monet's son Jean, in 1914 was a shattering blow. Worse still, Monet began to suffer increasingly from cataracts. It became harder for him to work outside in the garden, so instead, urged on by his great friend Georges Clemenceau, he built a large new studio to the right of the house and began painting the giant canvases, donated to France in April 1922 as *Les Décorations des Nymphéas*. These great, almost abstract masterpieces were painted from memory rather than observation. Proust paid homage to Monet's great talent: '... flowers of the earth, also flowers of the water, these tender water-lilies which the master has painted so sublimely ...' Clemenceau called the Japanese water garden his friend's studio, but by now the painter's eye had no use for the reflecting mirror across the Chemin du Roy.

Claude Monet died early in December 1926. Clemenceau hurried from the south of France to pay a final farewell to his friend. Finding Monet's coffin draped with the traditional black pall, he tore away the offensive cloth and seized a bright multi-coloured shawl to cover the coffin, saying '*Pas de noir pour Monet*'.

Blanche Monet stayed on at Giverny after Monet's death, keeping the house and garden as it had been during the painter's life. Monet's

Monet grew clematis on metal frames near the third studio built for his series *Les Décorations des Nymphéas*.

ABOVE White- and blue-flowering wisterias cover the Japanese bridge. OPPOSITE Climbing roses will soon cover the arches over the broad central avenue in the Clos Normand. As in Monet's day, nasturtiums blur the gravel walk with colour.

heir, his second son Michel, had always had a difficult relationship with his father, which in part explains why he never lived in the house and did nothing to keep it up or save the garden when his sister-in-law died after the war. But, by willing the property to the Académie des Beaux-Arts, he unknowingly brought about the rebirth of Giverny. Gerald van der Kemp's acceptance of the curatorship was the key element in this miracle. M. van der Kemp, already Curator of Versailles, hesitated before agreeing to his colleague's request, for Michel Monet left no financial provision for restoration or upkeep. But his admiration for Monet, coupled perhaps with the fact that he too is a painter and a gardener, persuaded him to undertake the task. Thanks

to his energy and dedication and to the help of his American wife, Florence, the long sad years of neglect ended. Monsieur Gilbert Vahé, a brilliant student at the Ecole Nationale d'Horticulture, became head gardener, and valuable help was given by all those who had known the garden in Monet's lifetime. All the available documents, including bills for plants and photographs of the garden, were used to restore the world of Claude Monet, and the Académie des Beaux-Arts has now opened Giverny to the public. But Giverny was never really a 'private' garden: Monet opened it to the world with the first paintings he made in his beloved garden, filling the garden with splendid colour, just as colour invaded and overflowed on to his canvases.

Le Pavillon de Fantaisie

Thury-Harcourt, near Alençon
(Le Duc et la Duchesse d'Harcourt)

THE PAVILLON DE FANTAISIE was built in 1753 by the Comte de Lillebonne, later the Duc d'Harcourt. Set in the park of Harcourt, some distance from the château, the building was used as a small orangery, a dairy and a pleasure pavilion for entertainments. A charming parterre lay in front of the building, which overlooks the valley of the Orne. It was here that Fragonard painted his well-known work, the series of *Figures de Fantaisie*, which featured the Duc d'Harcourt and his brother, the Duc de Beuvron, dressed as characters from the Italian *Commedia dell' arte*.

Thury-Harcourt was completely destroyed during the Second World War: nothing was left of the château, its park and gardens, for the floral terraces of the eighteenth century had become one of the battlefields of Normandy. It was here that the Duc and Duchesse d'Harcourt decided to create a new style of garden.

The *pavillon*, which had become a gardener's cottage in the nineteenth century, was enlarged and restored as their residence. Then they progressively integrated the new garden with the park, turning it into a harmonious composition which they opened to the public. The work involved in restoring the park was deeply satisfying, and the new spirit of the post-war period was to determine the character of the new layout. A number of grassed walks were cut into the park. Their names evoke spring: the wild cherry walk, the periwinkle walk, and the May walk, bordered with viburnum, syringa, cytisus, forsythia and Japanese cherries. Orderly red-flowering chestnut trees punctuate the landscape, and the open fields are starred with white narcissus and thickly planted with many varieties of daffodil. In spring the woodlands are carpeted with countless blue *Anemone blanda*, July brings the heavy scent of flowering privet, and in autumn the woods are coloured with the cherry-red-tinged leaves of the sumachs. An arbour leads to the banks of the Orne, where a delightful two-mile walk follows the river.

The summer garden is not immediately visible: a narrow path leads past a bank planted with spring-flowering periwinkles and autumn cyclamens to a wooden gate and a sloping shady walk beyond. As you round the last corner, the sudden unexpected view of the garden is breathtaking.

It is a large open area, marked off and outlined with trees. Poplars were planted to provide a fast-growing windbreak, thickened with a variety of conifers and underplanted with spring-flowering shrubs, chosen for scent as well as foliage colour – lilacs, red hawthorns and philadelphus. The main axis of the garden has been emphasized by four stone benches, salvaged from the great formal flight of steps leading to the château, which was destroyed by fire in 1944 during the battle of Normandy.

The entire area, now sheltered from the wind, was grassed and four long rectangular beds were cut out of the lawn. Pink- and blue-flowering hibiscus grow in the corners of the four beds, while the centres are filled with compositions of warm and luminous colours: the pale pink antirrhinum 'Floralis', *Salvia farinacea* and red-flowering malope. Colour harmonies change yearly as new varieties succeed older ones: bright zinnias, powder-blue ageratum, fragrant stock, sedum, antirrhinums, low growing verbena to edge the borders and long-flowering lavatera. The dwarf bronze-foliaged dahlia 'Redskin', which

The choice of colours in the long borders forms a large part of the careful yearly calculations. The successive flowering of the delphiniums and the asters, each planted out in irregular groups, adds blue to the garden, with white flowers juxtaposed to avoid any possible note of melancholy.

withstands both wet and dry spells, is used for ground cover, and this year the garden includes round cushions of impatiens (busy Lizzie) and spidery cleome. Silver-leaved plants or white flowers separate the strong colour groups, so as to maintain the garden's careful harmony.

Despite the enormous variety of colour and form, the scale of the planting avoids any impression of confusion. Each flower group fills a minimum of five square feet in the border, and the garden is more a carefully calculated disorder than an orderly confusion. Various cosmos, phlox, delphiniums, mallows and coreopsis create a tall central spine, against which the lower-growing plants are carefully placed. Is this the 'happy garden' the Duc d'Harcourt describes in the following passage from his book *Des Jardins Heureux*?

Architecture, painting, music and philosophy each have their place in the creation of a beautiful garden. Design and layout are a form of architecture; painting inspires the choice of colours; the rhythm of the garden can be compared to harmony in music; and lastly, the empty spaces belong to the field of philosophy.

Roses provide the permanent element in this ephemeral garden of annuals. The many varieties to be found in the borders include the well-known 'Queen Elizabeth' and 'Centenaire de Lourdes', and also the more unusual cherry-red 'Florian', the old-fashioned fragrant shrub rose 'Celeste', the lemon-yellow 'Casque d'Or', and the vigorous cyclamen-pink 'Lancôme', all of which deserve to be more widely used in modern gardens. The prolific Meilland family is present in force – 'Papa Meilland', 'Madame', 'Michèle' and 'Sonia'.

Flowers are chosen more for their contribution to the general design than for their rarity, and personal preferences are often sacrificed to this aim, for, as Paul Valéry wrote, 'What is beautiful is also tyrannical'. Certain plants were seen to be too high for the overall scheme and were suppressed, as were the superb dahlias, whose huge flower-heads were overwhelmed in the general picture. Jarring effects are avoided: for example, the traditional mixture of blue ageratum, yellow calceolaria and red salvia – favourites in every municipal garden in France – has no place in the subtler compositions at Thury-Harcourt.

The Duc and Duchesse have unified the garden with the addition of a terrace between the summer garden and the higher rose garden around the Pavillon de Fantaisie. The three separate elements are now joined to form a unit in the 175 acres of parkland, and the park itself flows into the natural landscape of the countryside.

The bank between the *pavillon* and the newly grassed terrace is a mixed border of spring- and summer-flowering plants, the two seasonal zones separated by ground-cover plants: hypericums, periwinkles and the golden *Juni-perus aurea*. Garden irises are useful on the bank, as they keep their lanceolate leaves in winter, oxalis provides an abundance of lovely small pink flowers and interesting foliage up to the first frosts, and rock roses bloom in profusion, including the good crimson-scarlet varieties. Here, as in the summer garden, varieties are often changed.

A subtle bond exists between the three banked terraces: they share either a repetitive or a complementary colour scheme. The owners carefully avoid monotony by adding a touch of the unexpected: each year at least one new plant variety is added – a modification which may change the overall harmony of the layout, but never unbalances it. When mistakes occur, they are corrected the following year, though slight imperfections do have an element of charm and human fallibility.

A successful garden, as described in *Des Jardins Heureux*, must not be the result of whim or fancy. A truly original creation depends upon fidelity to the precepts of layout and design; the planting-out of the garden should harmonize with the nature of the site and the natural landscape – in short, a garden should be faithful to the spirit of the place.

OPPOSITE Multicoloured borders cross a green carpet in the summer garden.
ABOVE Airy cosmos balanced by solid hollyhocks in a border.

Vauville

Beaumont-sur-Hague, near Cherbourg
(Madame Pellerin)

THE CHATEAU OF VAUVILLE rises, surrounded by a wall, from the middle of grazing lands barely 500 yards from the sea, facing west on the windswept point of the Cotentin peninsula.

In 1947, Eric and Nicole Pellerin decided to make a garden around the house on their family estate. As always with such a decision, problems followed. The only available protection (though insufficient) against the violent and frequent winds was the surrounding wall and a slight depression in the ground – remains of the old moat. The adjacent fields slope gently towards the sea, and seemed to admit no possibility of change.

The violence of the persistent west wind was the major handicap, but the climate could be counted on to balance the situation. The coast is warmed, like Cornwall and the Channel Islands, by a branch of the Gulf Stream – a benefit which made the creation of a botanical garden feasible.

A trip around the world left the Pellerins deeply impressed by the beauty of the landscape and tropical vegetation of Sri Lanka, and gradually the wild dream of a botanical garden at Vauville began to take shape.

Before starting their ambitious project the Pellerins decided on the following guide lines. Firstly, it should be a 'natural', spontaneous garden: a *jardin à la française* would be out of place on this rough coast, and an English garden, even when designed and laid out by a master, often reveals a discernible degree of artifice. They would plant only evergreens, so that it would be a garden for all seasons. The nature of the site would be fully used without modification, except for the new planting. The gardens reserved for delicate plants would be bordered by wind-resistant hedges, composed of a mixture of exotic or unusual shrubs. Grassed paths would be used in place of ordered avenues, and a few low stone walls would separate natural areas from the planted garden. Finally, large concentrations of plants would add botanical interest to the garden, so as to avoid a sampling of unrelated plants.

The result is neither a park nor a garden in the formal sense of the word; it is rather a subtropical oasis. A visit to Vauville clearly shows that no professional gardener or landscape architect would have undertaken such a project: innocence, and optimism as strong and steady as the prevailing winds, and a con-fidence in the ability of the plants to survive, were all necessary ingredients in making the garden.

Planting was started in the old moat, a natural windbreak. Elsewhere, other windbreaks were begun. Shrubs were planted for the spectacular nature of their foliage: large beds of *Gynerium argenteum*, *Phormium tenax*, like giant ten-foot irises, sharp-bladed eryngium, and decorative *Cordyline australis*, mixed with trachycarpus, the fern palm, in concentrated groups or belts. None was staked, even in the earliest years, for Eric Pellerin considered that staking, even on this windswept land, was to be avoided, for it encouraged plants to grow lazy. They should be made to resist the force of the wind with their own strength.

The first view of the garden is surprising. Plants are laid out in broad belts encircling empty grassed areas, with ten-foot-high hedges of deep pink escalonias, and in some places there are 500-foot-long swathes of eryngium. The flora of the Mediterranean flourishes in this climate, for the natural humidity of the Cotentin replaces the need for water, and in winter the temperature rarely falls below freezing. Even the most tender species grow easily, sheltered by the windbreaks. *Echium piriana*, a native of the Canary Islands with spectacular blue flowers, grows to fifteen feet before dying after its flowering period. These giant plants have a two-year lifespan, but spontaneously re-seed themselves to assure their own survival. There are dense plantings of *Beschorneria yuc-coides*, too irregular to be called borders, and oases of trachycarpus, Canary Island phoenix and *Cordyline australis* (a plant often confused with dracæna), with dense clusters of leaves

OPPOSITE The Château of Vauville, rising from a subtropical landscape. ABOVE Shrubs native to the Mediterranean flourish at Vauville. They are chosen for their spectacular foliage.

Giant gunnera with leaves up to nine feet across border the canal.

crowning each branch. There are over 300 of these tree-plants in the garden and more are planted every year. The sea-spray resistant cordyline has a fascinating survival technique: should its trunk be damaged, broken, cracked or flattened by the wind, a new stem emerges from the base of the plant. These plants were grown from seed gathered from the first ones to be planted at Vauville, and now, backed by eucalyptus, bamboos and fig trees, form a belt around large empty areas and create shelter for camellias and rhododendrons, planted in soil specially prepared with added peat. Chemical fertilizers and all pesticides are banned at Vauville (though the fields were nevertheless enriched by the herds of Norman catttle long before the garden was planted), but the size to which these subtropicals grow in a sheltered oasis is astounding.

Of all these Mediterranean-type plants, only the daturas are given winter indoor protection. Mimosa perfumes the garden, and cistus, euphorbia, agave, orange and lemon trees and even a banana tree, which bears no fruit owing to the cool climate, remain outdoors all year. Certain plants were skilfully positioned by the Pellerins to harmonize with the colour of the shale roof of the nearby house, and a splendid group of acanthus, yucca, eucalyptus and other grey-leaved plants adds to the composition. Sections of the garden are used for various different planting schemes, separated and pro-

tected by the screening hedges The dominant flowers in the garden – agapanthus, tritonias, arums, hemerocallis, *Lobelia cardinalis*, echium, beschorneria and yuccoides, all plants with spectacular flowers – were chosen to complement the architecture of these sheltered areas.

Running water in canals half-hidden behind the high vegetation mirror large glowing groups of double-flowering blue and violet *Iris kæmpferi*. Osmunda, the superb royal fern, grows with massed deep pink crinum in the island beds.

The giant gunnera in other gardens cannot compare with the astonishing ramparts of the plant that border the length of this 300-foot canal, each leaf between six and nine feet across.

The history of these exotic plants, now thriving in unlikely Normandy, how they were obtained and their arrival at Vauville, is an intriguing story. Amazingly, not one plant was bought, for as Nicole Pellerin explains, the garden was created by a system of 'barter or gift'. Eucalyptus from New Zealand, for example, were gained in exchange for French lettuce seeds, and there were precious gifts of seed from garden lovers in other lands. Most of the plants at Vauville are natives of the southern hemisphere: Eric Pellerin instinctively realized their potential for adaptation, and managed to obtain cuttings and seeds from various botanical gardens. Now, thirty years later, the garden is almost autonomous: the plants are propagated from seed, cuttings or division. After much work done with great care, the gardens of Vauville give a strong impression of 'otherness'; it is a surprising and unique garden, an explosion of self-perpetuating vegetation, the transformation of a poet's dream into a botanist's reality.

Since her husband's recent death, Madame Pellerin has continued his work with the help of two gardeners and her children, who have found homes in the village close to the family château. The gardens of Vauville, where each group of plant is all-important, have the naïve charm of a painting by Douanier Rousseau. The unexpected splendour of the vegetation, orderly but natural, achieves the supreme goal of making the visitor forget the art with which it was accomplished.

All the plants at Vauville are grown from cuttings or seeds obtained by a system of 'barter or gift'.

Kerdalo

Tredarzec
(Le Prince Wolkonsky)

IT WAS love at first sight when Peter Wolkonsky discovered Kerdalo near the village of Tredarzec in 1962, where he was to use all his talents – as painter, architect, stonemason and gardener – in the creation of this garden in Brittany. Wolkonsky's previous garden on the heights of Saint-Cloud, outside Paris, was in the classical Italian mode, with geometrical parterres of lilies and delphiniums bordered with box, the mandatory fountains, carved stone urns, and a formal stonebordered pond. The contrast between Saint-Cloud and Kerdalo, therefore, is total. Moreover, Saint-Cloud was on chalk, and had no natural water; the soil at Kerdalo is acid, and there are several natural springs. Apart from its natural beauty, Kerdalo is interesting in many ways, for it is a modern garden, still in the process of creation. Laid out on terrain chosen primarily for the acidity of the soil, it is a rarity: a site chosen for a garden rather than a garden adapted to the existing site.

'My dream', says Wolkonsky, 'was to grow azaleas, rhododendrons, camellias, magnolias … everything I couldn't grow on the chalk at Saint-Cloud. And I wanted a water garden with astilbes and rodgersia'. So he went in search of the ideal site with spring water in a climate congenial to his plants, eventually finding a broken-down farmhouse with thirty-five acres of land near the Channel coast of Brittany. The land was too uneven for modern methods of agriculture, and had become uneconomical for farming, but he was at work on it even before the contract was signed.

Surprisingly, he made no overall plans for planting, relying on inspiration, adapting the planting to the plants at hand, season by season, and landscaping as he went. Kerdalo is the creation of an insatiable gardener, always searching for new mediums and effects: a garden of woodland and water, shrubs and herbaceous borders, bogs and dry banks, marshland and valley planting, elegant pavilions and excellent stone terrace-work.

Peter Wolkonsky's first concern was to plant trees. Most garden plants are easily transplanted, but trees can never be moved; for this reason he insists that they should be planted in their definitive, permanent position. All the trees at Kerdalo were planted young – a great many directly from seed – and they receive special protection to ensure sound rooting during their first two years. The first to be planted (in 1964) were to serve as windbreaks: *Chamæcyparis lawsoniana* 'Aurea', *Pinus radiata* and *Quercus ilex*, the evergreen oak. All were sown from seed in their permanent positions, and now they are over thirty feet high.

Trees were planted not only for wind protection, but also for special foliage effects. The uneven land offers many possibilities for achieving interesting effects, for instance the group of gold- and silver-leaved shrubs which, planted in front of a distant colonnade of dark cypresses on the hillside overlooking the gardens, create a glorious flaming effect in the light of the setting sun: gold and silver hollies, golden euonymus and pittosporums, *Taxus baccata* 'Standishii', the best of the golden yews, the russet-purple *Berberis thunbergii* 'Atropurpurea Nana', and the 'burning bush', *Cotinus coggygria purpureus*. Wherever he uses deciduous trees, Peter Wolkonsky is careful to plant evergreens nearby to assure permanent foliage colour: the collection of azaleas is backed by a group of conifers and other evergreen shrubs to add extra interest after their spectacular spring show: and elsewhere, a *Cornus controversa*, planted near its striking silver variegated form, is interesting both aesthetically and botanically. Colour is not the only criterion in the planting schemes: the horizontal growth of *Abies koreana* and *Podocarpus macrophylla* planted in a group of a dozen or so trees illustrates a particular concern with form and habits of growth.

The house stands between two gardens so totally dissimilar that one might think they had been planted in different climates. Behind lies the sun garden, on a steep bank cut into a series of sheltered terraces where the planting is Mediterranean. The grassed paths are edged with abutilon, *Cytisus racemosus*, clumps of lavender, bright gazanias and silvery-white clumps of *Convolvulus cneorum*. Tall spikes of the

ABOVE Gunnera in the water garden.

ABOVE RIGHT Alternate squares of grass and pebbles show a Japanese influence.

PREVIOUS PAGES RIGHT The gardens are laid out on a series of terraces in front of the house.

PREVIOUS PAGES LEFT Ethiopian zantedeschia reflected in the water.

Mexican *Beschorneria yuccoides* soar above a collection of phormium and massed blue-flowered *Echium pinninana*. In spring, two enormous sixteen-foot-high *Drimys winteri* make a stunning picture on a lower level, their abundant ivory-white flowers sweeping the ground. The parent plants of these drimys are in the garden of the Vicomte de Noailles in Grasse (pp 202–11).

In front of the house a large retaining wall, encrusted with plants, divides two broad terraces filled with a variety of silver-leaved aromatic plants. The higher terrace bordering the house is paved with pebbles set in cement – far prettier and more interesting than the dreary gravel that surrounds most French houses. The border against the house is rich in lilies, nerine, *Amaryllis belladonna* and *Libertia formosa*. Pinks blur the straight line of the border, their silver-grey foliage blending with the colour of the pebbled terrace. Two handsome *Raphiolepsis × delacourii*, evergreen rounded shrubs discovered in China, with glossy leaves and rose-pink flowers in April, frame the entrance door. These, together with the *Vallea stipularis* growing against the wall, received an award at the Cornwall flower show at Truro in 1978.

Among the many beauties at Kerdalo per-haps the most spectacular are the ceanothus, some of which have grown to tree-like propor-tions. The twelve-year-old *Ceanothus impressus* covers some ten square yards of the house façade with thousands of deep blue flowers. In March a *Clematis armandii* festoons the façade with white blooms, and the large-flowered, highly scented climbing rose 'Madame Gré-goire Staechelin' is a summer glory.

A double staircase leads down to the lower garden, called the four squares, which is charmingly informal. A mixture of silver-leaved perennials, nepeta, flowering shrubs, euphorbias and roses share the space in har-monious anarchy, with the rare and beautiful summer- to early autumn-flowering tree, *Eucryphia lucida × cordifolia* marking the corners of the beds.

The fountain and terrace are in the Italian style; two corner pavilions have charming murals depicting birds in a mosaic of shells and coloured stones, created in a frenzied race by Peter Wolkonsky and a most talented friend, Nicole des Forêt, each working in 'their' pavilion.

A wide path in a chequered pattern of pebbles and grass makes a splendid transition between the formalized symmetry of the higher terrace and the romantic garden below. On the

higher level a long narrow pool stretches behind a Chinese pagoda designed by the owner. Hemerocallis, hostas and agapanthus fill a thick, compact border near an excellent collection of *Rhododendron augustinii*, a fast-growing blue-flowered Chinese species, perhaps the finest of all rhododendrons. A group of hydrangeas adds to this unforgettable study in blue.

Every level of ground at Kerdalo is constructed so as to give an individual character to each view. The springs at the top of the valley have been channelled between banks heavily planted with rhododendrons, the pale cream and yellow flowers beautifully reflected in the water. Among the many varieties along the bank are the two remarkable Exbury hybrids with huge bell-shaped flowers, 'China' and 'Crest', and another beautiful *Eucryphia lucida × cordifolia*, pruned into a conical shape, thrives on the moist ground. Peter Wolkonsky plans to plant an avenue of these superb ornamental evergreen trees.

The pond in the heart of a deep valley is another of Kerdalo's *pièces de resistance*. The banks are planted with massed groups of azaleas, pieris and camellias growing in the half-shade, and dense and colourful clusters of *Primula japonica*, *Lysichiton americanus*, the majestic *Ligularia dentata* and the graceful *Cimicifuga racemosa* at the water's edge. *Camellia reticulata*, *Camellia williamsii* and their hybrids have been planted on the hillside. (Peter Wolkonsky dislikes and avoids all the *Camellia japonica*: their faded flowers stuck to the branches make an ungainly sight.)

Hydrangea petiolaris and *Rosa* 'Wedding Day' cover the rough trunks of some of the larger trees in the valley, and sprays of white flowers hang from the branches of other trees. Spring finds the valley carpeted with primulas and hellebores, while clouds of blue 'Headbourne' hybrid agapanthus, freely planted in large groups, flower later in the season. Normally agapanthus are formally grouped in the garden; here, mixed with *Hosta sieboldiana*, they grow in spontaneous abundance, and the effect is wild and exuberant.

Although Peter Wolkonsky is an ardent collector, Kerdalo avoids the contrived look of most botanical parks. Each plant, shrub and tree fits into its logical setting, forming a harmonious picture in spite of the wide diversity of architectural styles and plant varieties. Water, stone and plants are perfectly integrated with each other, the architect's art and the painter's eye making a perfect marriage of form and colour.

ABOVE LEFT and RIGHT Peter Wolkonsky's dream was 'to grow rhododendrons, camellias, magnolias . . . everything I couldn't grow on the chalk at St-Cloud. And I wanted a water garden with astilbes and rodgersia.'

Parc Floral d'Apremont

near Nevers

(La Société Hôtelière d'Apremont)

IN THE MIDDLE AGES, generations of families from the village of Apremont found work in the surrounding quarries. The stone was loaded on to long flat barges and floated down the river Allier to the Loire, where it was used to build some of the most beautiful churches in Orléans. It was also used for the small houses of the village, typical of the Berry area.

In 1930 Eugène Schneider, captivated by the romantic dream of restoring Apremont to its medieval appearance, began with the help of the architect, M. de Galéa, the long, patient reconstruction of the village. Most of the houses date from the fifteenth, sixteenth and seventeenth centuries, and anything built later

was unwanted. Offending buildings were razed to the ground, and whole groups of houses were rebuilt in the medieval style of Berry, with roofs of flat Burgundian tiles and walls coloured ochre with a wash of sand and lime.

The owners of the château have continued this work. In 1971 Gilles de Brissac, a French landscape architect with a growing reputation, began to plan the Parc Floral, a project destined to include the small, sleepy village in a large tourist plan. Since the war, the average Frenchman has become increasingly interested in small-scale gardening, learning more about plants and where and how to use them. Apremont's cottage gardens and the new Parc

The medieval village beyond a corner of the garden.

Floral could become a living lesson in gardening, with something for every taste.

The future park had been pasture land for cattle, and the lawns undoubtedly benefited from this accumulation of natural fertilizer when they were laid. But the first step before any planting was done was to create a continuous series of pools by damming the upper valley. A waterfall was built to form the centre of the garden, using 600 tons of rock – enormous slabs brought in by lorry from the old quarries at neighbouring Sancoins. A closed-circuit system using two submerged pumps keeps the water in continuous motion. The waterfall is surrounded by a vast rock garden planted mainly with low-growing horizontal conifers, iris and various primulas, and the water flows through three pools planted with lotus and water-lilies. Only when all this had been done were lawns laid and groves of shrubs planted.

Trees were brought in, weighing from three to four tons, and bulldozed into position. The most interesting conifers are the striking columnar incense cedar, *Calocedrus decurrens*, the small-coned *Cryptomeria japonica*, and the *Ginkgo biloba* – the last survivor of an ancient family of trees once thought extinct and a tree of great beauty, with fan-shaped leaves which turn a lovely yellow in autumn. The dawn redwood, *Metasequoia glyptostroboides*, which loses its leaves in winter, and the giant Californian 'Wellingtonia', *Sequoiadendron giganteum*, some species of which have lived over 3,000 years, are also worthy of note.

The park boasts a fine plantation of *Eucalyptus gunnii* and *Magnolia grandiflora*, but perhaps the loveliest trees are the deciduous collection chosen for their autumn foliage. A decorative group of acacias, including the rose acacia *Robinia hispida*, grows near the shade of the red horse chestnut, *Aesculus × carnea* 'Briottii' bearing large rose-pink panicles in spring. Birch groves are light green in May and shimmering yellow in October. The paper birch, *Betula papy-*

The waterfall, in the rock garden. The conifers and bog garden plants had just been planted when this photograph was taken.

The laburnum pergola creates a long, half-shaded garden walk.

rifera, and the dome-shaped weeping birch, *Betula pendula* 'Youngii', thrive here. The bright berries of small flowering thorn trees, such as *Cratægus oxyacantha* 'Paul's Scarlet' and *Cratægus × Lavallei* shine crimson in winter. In addition, the park has a number of majestic European and Asiatic beeches, including the spectacular weeping beech and variegated-leaved varieties such as *Fagus sylvatica* 'Roseomarginata', with purple leaves bordered with pale pink. Lovely sweet gums, *Liquidambar styraciflua*, with crimson leaves in autumn, and the fast-growing North American tulip tree, *Liriodendron tulipifera*, are reaching maturity along with many varieties of flowering cherries, and slow-growing oaks are an investment for the future.

A long pergola runs across the park, creating a long half-shaded garden walk. Golden laburnums flower through the trellises in spring, followed by white Japanese wisteria and rose-flowering acacias. The beds and borders are filled with massed hardy perennials in large groups of contrasting colours.

Apremont is one of the few gardens in France that can boast a large collection of white-flowering and silver-leaved plants, planted in a special border inspired by the 'white garden' at Sissinghurst.

Gilles de Brissac is a perfectionist, and his own severest critic. It takes time – at least three or four years – to discover which plants succeed best in a garden, and it takes courage for the owner to steel himself to remove the failures. Apremont is now in a period of transition: the basic structure remains the same – the waterfall, canals, hedges and trees – but the choice of shrubs and bedding-out plants is being reconsidered.

Greater importance is being given to ground-cover plants, and to the summer-flowering bulbs that have proved so successful at Apremont: tropical *Crocosmia masonorum*, montbretia and *Crinum × powellii*. These have replaced many of the low-growing conifers, which were too numerous. The flat, uninteresting rose beds, like the ones often to be seen on the forecourts of French petrol stations, have also disappeared, together with the lavender and rosemary bushes, which did not do well in the climate of Berry.

Elsewhere, some varieties bedded out in the spring and summer borders and even in the white garden have been reduced by half. All the replacements, tested at Apremont over the two previous summers, appear to be real improvements. In the white garden, the *Leucanthemum* 'Etoile d'Anvers' has been replaced by the German variety 'Schwabengruss', a far better plant, and the 'Iceberg' floribunda roses have been increased from twenty to two hundred, replacing the exuberant rugosa, 'Blanc Double de Coubert', which took up too much space, and 'Madame Plantier', one of Gertrude Jekyll's favourites which, alas, is non-recurrent. *Philadelphus* 'Virginal' also lost its place, owing to its stiff habit of growth: it is far more effective in bouquets than in the border.

In the spring garden the Jerusalem sage, *Phlomis fruticosa*, which had become too large and invasive to the detriment of its neighbours, was removed, as was the old rose 'Jacques Cartier', whose faded-pink flowers have the unfortunate habit of falling after even the slightest of showers. New, more dominant varieties were added to the border, including the eglantine-type shrub rose 'Cocktail', which is covered with yellow-centred geranium-red blooms from June until the first frosts.

The back of the larger summer border was reinforced with a number of vigorous shrubs, including *Cotinus coggygria* 'Flame', *Cornus controversa* 'Variegata', a number of rugosa roses chosen for the density of their foliage rather than for their flowers, *Choisya ternata*, *Sambucus nigra* 'Aurea' (a yellow-green elder), *Syringa* 'Bellicent' and 'MacFarlane' (both late-blooming lilacs), *Echinacea purpurea* 'Abend-sonne' (the purple cone flower closely related to rudbeckia, and a strong plant resistant to

both wind and weather), and *Coreopsis lanceolata* 'Sonnenkind', a compact plant with a long flowering period. As the number of plant varieties has been reduced throughout the garden, striking new colour has been added.

Three new projects have been started. A group of fine *Eucalyptus gunnii* has been established in a large border, following the success of a single specimen in surviving the harshest winters. The young trees are a startling silver-blue and can be pruned into an excellent bush. Rustic bamboos have been planted near the waterfall, and this spring water-lilies were added to the first canal, protected by wire from the greed of the aquatic birds living in the park, which had destroyed the first planting.

Sparing neither time nor expense, and taking unlimited trouble, Gilles de Brissac has created at Apremont the only privately owned garden in France designed for the public and laid out for the pleasure of others.

Cleomes dominate a pretty confusion of plants in this cottage garden in the village.

Château de Touffou

near Chauvigny
(Mr and Mrs David Ogilvy)

THE CHÂTEAU OF TOUFFOU, perched high on an artificial spur over the river Vienne, made its first historical appearance in 1127 under the name of *Tolfol*, when it was in the possession of the powerful Oger family. The old stone of the six large turreted stone buildings is a worn apricot-ochre colour, the turrets are roofed in blue-grey slate, and together they form a happy equilibrium in spite of the diversity of architectural styles. The guard tower dates from the twelfth century, the dungeon – undoubtedly the work of an Oger – from the thirteenth. There is a Renaissance wing, and the turrets are a typical nineteenth-century addition.

Maurice Garçon of the French Academy wrote of Touffou:

For the most part very old castles find a place in history through wars and battles. One must use one's imagination to reconstruct the stages of successive change through a tangled web of architectural styles or the desolation of ruins. Miraculously, Touffou avoided the normal setbacks of time. The various modifications of the château were all due to the changing tastes of its owners within the framework of the style of the period. This group of magnificent buildings built over a long span of time to protect its inhabitants from siege and the hazards of combat, served to shelter a happy and peaceful way of life. The history of Touffou is traced in the architectural work and stones of the castle.

In 1964 this historic monument was placed on

The lawn above the river is bordered by cedars.

the market by its then owner, Enguerand de Vergie. David Ogilvy, an ardent Francophile of Scottish descent who had spent many happy holidays touring France by bicycle, decided to buy it and save it from certain ruin, for the foundations were unsound and the roof was badly in need of repair. Touffou was shrouded in scaffolding for years before at last emerging restored and rejuvenated. The castle walls are mellow with the warm patina of time and the new English-style gardens add to the beauty of the place. It is the realization of a dream which once must have appeared quite incompatible with the active life of an international businessman.

David Ogilvy was sixty years old when he decided to exchange the frenetic life he led as the President of Ogilvy and Mather, one of the largest advertising agencies in the world with over a hundred offices in thirty-five countries, for a quiet retreat in Poitou. (He has, however,

installed a telex in a corner of the twelfth-century library.)

He dreamt of a garden. When he bought Touffou, the only semblance of a garden was the gravelled *cour d'honneur*, laid out with box parterres and a few grassed squares. The park and walled kitchen garden lay beyond the *enceinte* of the castle, near the stables and out-buildings. What form would it take, the first garden to be designed by a sexagenarian Scot in a French historical framework? An English-style garden attached to this very French château might seem anachronistic, but some-how it has worked – the atmosphere very definitely derives from English gardening con-cepts developed in the early twentieth century. A series of garden rooms, enclosed between high hedges, are freely and informally planted with a wide variety of plants. Harmonies of scent and colour, a deep sense of rhythm and exquisite taste vanquish all regrets for the

High above the river Vienne the twelfth-century tower overlooks the formally planted lower terrace.

Juniperus chamaecyparis planted near a large shrub rose 'Stanwell Perpetual' makes an unexpected sight on the lawn.

traditional flat symmetries of the classic French garden.

David Ogilvy is a man who seeks and obtains rapid results in life, and gardening is no exception. He decided to use thuya to make the hedges on which the structure of the garden depends, rather than the traditional slow-growing yew, and now the hedges have the volume and proportions of a second gener-ation wall of yew.

The new garden is laid out in the old kitchen garden, totally invisible from the house and separate from it. This is a complete break with

the French tradition of the château garden as an extension of the house, to be viewed from inside by guests not too anxious to dirty their shoes. Touffou is a garden to wander through: the planting is informal and unrestrained, with old roses, lavender, lilies and santolina planted together and framed by green lawns.

Touffou is a classified historic monument and so permission had to be obtained from the relevant authorities before digging the swim-ming pool. Permission was accorded but only on the condition that the swimming pool remained totally invisible from the castle.

David Ogilvy satisfied this condition by creating a curious optical illusion: the land slopes up towards the pool, making the water invisible as you enter the garden, so that people bathing appear as severed heads rolling across the lawn. In fact, one of Ogilvy's guests fainted with fear when confronted by the extraordinary sight of a head rolling along the end of the lawn: the

only possible explanation seemed to be that it was a garden ghost from the past.

Old roses dominate the garden. *Rosa filipes* 'Kiftsgate' and the equally rampant cascading *Rosa* 'Wedding Day' climb through the old apple and cherry trees. The pale blush-pink 'Cuisse de Nymphe Emue' or 'Maiden's Blush', 'Blanc Double de Coubert' and the six-foot

Blue and pink delphiniums bordered by *Nepeta mussinii*.

RIGHT White-flowering annuals set in box-bordered squares with a backdrop of clipped thuyas.
ABOVE The entrance to the garden is through high thuya hedges.

double carmine-pink alba, *Rosa* 'Königin von Dänemark' back the traditional long herbaceous border. The front borders are planted with silver, shrubby, sweet-smelling artemisias, nepetas, rock roses and mints. The stone walls of the old kitchen garden are mostly covered with climbing roses: the first to bloom, in April, is the small golden-flowered 'Canary Bird', followed by one of the best of the modern shrub roses, the arching creamy-yellow-flowered 'Frühlingsgold', heavy with perfume. The marvellous climber *Rosa* 'Mermaid', with eglantine-shaped pale yellow flowers and virtually evergreen leaves, covers the east wall of the garden, and the blood-red *Rosa moyesii* has grown to fourteen feet up the chapel walls. For two weeks in June a dozen 'Madame Grégoire Stæchelin' make an extraordinary show against another of the old stone walls. This rose has a brief but unforgettable flowering season, when it envelops the wall with a cloud of pink flowers.

David Ogilvy is justifiably proud of his long hedge of ceanothus, which he planted himself from seed: it flowered after only six years and is already ten feet high. The most impressive sight in the garden is the 200-year-old holly with a five-foot circumference.

'Trevithian' daffodils star the lawn in spring, their delicate scent a delight so early in the gardening season. Massed groups of *Romneya coulteri*, glistening paper-white California poppies, flower and prosper in the soft climate of Poitou. They are not unknown in French gardens, but never in the quantity one sees here at Touffou. Appropriately, this very English garden ends in a croquet lawn, each corner marked with an elegant weeping silver *Pyrus salicifolia* 'Pendula'.

Although certain parts of the château are open to the public the garden is private, but if a visitor shows a particular interest David Ogilvy will almost certainly take pleasure in showing them round, as he did with a group of blind people drawn towards the garden by the wafts of perfume from the roses. 'I realized more than ever before', he says, 'the joy and importance of scent in the garden, scent not only from the flowers, but from the leaves you can crush between your fingers'.

The deep English border is filled with a profusion of silver-leaved plants and shrubs: *Stachys lanata*, *Pieris salicifolia*, rosemary and white-flowering shrub roses.

Château de Hautefort

near Périgueux
(La Baronne de Bastard)

'HAUTEFORT has the majesty of a royal castle', wrote André Maurois of this magnificent edifice rising high above its village to dominate the Périgord countryside. The château's origins are ancient. It was probably built on the site of a Roman camp, hence its name: *Altefortis*, then *Autafort*, *Autifort*, and finally Hautefort in the eighteenth century. Its first known châtelain was Guy de Lastours in the early eleventh century. One of his descendants followed Godefroy de Bouillon to Jerusalem in 1099, where legend tells that he saved a lion from an enormous serpent. The grateful beast attached himself to the young knight until he sailed back to France, when he plunged into the sea to paddle behind the ship until his strength failed and he drowned.

Two brothers held joint seignory over Hautefort between 1160 and 1169: the celebrated knight and troubadour, Bertrand de Born, and his brother Constantin. Bertrand, described by Dante as a 'sower of discord', had a bellicose nature and, annoyed by this forced cohabit-ation, expelled his brother and family. He also involved himself in the endless provincial battles between Henry II of England and Philippe Auguste of France, and played a dominant role in the wars between Henry, his sons and their mother, Eleanor of Aquitaine.

Prosperity and peace came to Hautefort at the end of the Hundred Years War, and little changed until the Renaissance, when the shape of the grim, medieval fortress was slightly altered. It assumed its present form in the seventeenth century, when Jacques-François de Hautefort commissioned the architect Nicolas Rambourg to modify the medieval building in the *grand siècle* style of the period.

The Revolution would have passed unevent-fully over Hautefort had not its naïve châte-lains rashly travelled to Paris, where they were seized and guillotined in 1794, during the Reign of Terror. Hautefort then became the property of their grand-daughter and her hus-band, the Baron de Damas, a great royalist. With their deaths the Hautefort family died

out and the château was sold. A period of neglect ensued when even the furniture was sold at public auction, to the shame and disgust of the village.

Baron and Baroness Henri de Bastard bought the property in 1929; by 1957, the year of the Baron's death, they had restored the château and created the new gardens. In 1968 catastrophe struck when a young, thoughtless guest carelessly dropped a lighted cigarette in the attic. In less than ten hours on the night of August 30th, Hautefort was reduced to a charred, smoking skeleton: the flames lit up the countryside for twenty miles around, and only the two tower wings escaped destruction. In the face of such a tragedy, the Baroness was determined to restore the whole castle, and thanks to her great courage and devotion to Hautefort, the work will soon be finished.

Perhaps this period of rebuilding has been beneficial for the gardens, a pause for thought and change. For the extraordinary grounds of Hautefort are an integral part of its beauty, their form and colour echo and contrast with the strong horizontal lines of the massive stone walls and the rounded, grey-blue tower roofs. The dominant colour is green, with generous use of bright bedding-out plants, but it is essentially a garden of dark yews – with a long green pergola in thuya – of formal box par-

Thirty-year-old box topiary echoes the rounded shape of the double dome of the chapel roof.

OPPOSITE ABOVE Low borders of variegated box filled with clipped yew lead the eye to the monumental castle. Topiary yews are being formed to add to the simple design.
OPPOSITE BELOW A group of topiary bordered with low box and dahlias.
FAR LEFT This box design in the south-east garden below the chapel represents the sun.
LEFT Alternating squares of white and red begonias form a simple pattern in the new garden under the now-restored north face of the castle.

terres and delightful box topiary bordering the wide entrance ramp and ornamenting the south-west garden.

The Baron de Bastard was an enthusiastic gardener. In 1929 Hautefort was a neglected nineteenth-century English-style park, with a few tired flower beds set in the patchy grass near the château and some flowering shrubs and trees scattered here and there. The park was tidied up and the remnants of the garden removed entirely – including the grass, for before the war the château had no permanent water supply and so a lawn could not be properly maintained. The Baron's first head gardener, M. Delaivier, trained M. Becker, who was to continue his work for a further thirty-five years and who, though nominally retired, still supervises the gardens and plans future changes. He is an excellent, tenacious, conscientious and, rarest of all, creative gardener. He remembers the Baron as a wonderful person to work for, 'a man who enjoyed innovation as much as I, who unhesitatingly provided the necessary workers for all the new projects'. Their collaboration was a happy one; only twice did they disagree. The first occasion was when the Baron replaced the lime avenue

with the long thuya pergola, a winter windbreak as well as a deliciously cool summer promenade that forms a closed tunnel seventy-five yards long. Only later were doors and side windows cut into it, and finally, ten years ago, to Becker's joy and relief, openings were cut in the roof to prevent the trees from dying back completely. The second point of disagreement was over the huge rose bed planted along the length of the pergola. Becker insisted that roses were never successful on lime and wholeheartedly disapproved of the Baron's beloved rose bed. One suspects that he already longed to begin designing and planting the formal box parterre which replaced the roses soon after the Baron's death. Cones and balls of clipped box grow high above the eighteenth-century design, breaking the horizontal monotony of the parterre and pergola. The two perfectly complement each other and the château beyond. Two smaller box parterres were recently added to the dry moat under the drawbridge: the larger forms a knot garden linking the letters H and S, Henri and Simone de Bastard's initials. Sometimes visitors mistake this tender alliance for the letters SOS, possibly imagining a sad reference to the fire of 1968.

ABOVE A knot garden in the dry moat to the left of the drawbridge links Henri and Simone de Bastard's initials.

RIGHT M. Becker, the semi-retired head gardener, continues to supervise all the garden designs and tend his nursery of young box topiary in the kitchen garden.

The south-east garden is best seen from the balustrade bordering the inner courtyard. Lean against the sun-warmed stone and look down on the garden framed by the red-tiled roofs of the village and the calm green countryside of Périgord. The central parterre is made up of three alternating designs: the sun (Périgord is sunny), a windmill (the château's position is windy), and a double scroll shape, with no obvious meaning. As the Baroness laughingly says, 'everything at Hautefort seems symbolic, but nothing is'. Symbolic or not, the designs are very effective. Santolina lends a touch of silver, while flowers fill the empty spaces. The planting scheme was inverted a few years ago, when box replaced the flowers in the parterres. As at Villandry, the parterres are replanted every spring and summer, and the plant varieties are changed annually. Red and white begonias replaced last year's geraniums, and forget-me-nots may be flowering there next year. Before the fire the high, massive castle wall was planted with grapevines; now they are covered with superb espaliered *Magnolia grandifloras*. The Baroness overcame Becker's stubborn conviction that they would never succeed on the rubble-covered stone foundations, and

now they flourish there. Becker, converted by this triumph, intends to espalier camellias against the north wall.

The garden facing south-east, behind the chapel, has the old-fashioned charm of the marvellous French parterres of the 1900s still to be seen in some seaside resorts; a faint memory of former taste and elegance. The ground here falls away from the centre and seems to be slipping into the landscape. The unevenness of the terrain creates a magical imbalance with the solid mass of the castle. The distant view of the surrounding countryside provides an unobtrusive misty backdrop to the garden. Becker once dreamed of creating an Italian garden here by levelling the ground into three terraces. Luckily this plan was abandoned, for the off-balance charm of the whole design would have been lost.

Parterres thickly edged in box fit their allotted spaces like pieces of a jigsaw puzzle, while the box topiary, always curiously and asymmetrically placed in the garden, seems to be playing children's games. Its positioning exaggerates the site's idiosyncrasies without

dully correcting them. Some, planted over thirty years ago, imitate the shape of the chapel's double dome. Bright anemone-type and small decorative dahlias, mostly yellow, fill the spaces between the low box hedges, and every year cuttings are taken to ensure a constant supply of replacements for diseased or worn-out plants. Only occasionally are they grown from seed, as the colours rarely come true. Wallflowers are planted out in spring, when masses of tree peonies, planted at the same time as the topiary, flower gloriously if briefly. One narrow outer border is planted in summer with the dark blue heliotrope, *Heliotropium* 'Lemoine's Giant', for its pervasive heady scent.

Becker is now mulling over the idea of replacing the dahlias in the central parterre with box, and he hopes to be able to add more topiary to give height to the back border against the château wall. All these plans are discussed with Madame de Bastard, who, with unfailing good humour, usually approves.

The north side of the château suffered most damage in the fire of 1968. Becker was sub-

Openings were cut in the roof of the 70 metre long thuya pergola to keep the trees healthy and provide alternating light and shade.

sequently delighted to be able to take advantage of this calamity by removing the border of hydrangeas that he never quite approved of, and beginning work on the new side garden in 1982. He laid out a long rectangular parterre running the length of the wall, edged in box and made up of alternating squares and rectangles of red and white begonias and blue ageratum. Clipped box spheres have been started in the nursery garden and will be added to the parterre when mature.

For anyone interested in the reverse side of the neat and perfect gardens of Hautefort, it is worth walking down the hill to the kitchen garden. The spirit of Villandry (pp 164–71) is very evident in this nursery, where yews, thuyas and box are all skilfully trained. It takes seven years of continuous attention to shape them, and as box is prone to attacks of rust, it needs to be sprayed every three weeks with a copper sulphate solution. For the treatment to be really effective, the plants have to be spread open with a rake during spraying.

A cast-iron pump near the old stone water trough is the centrepiece of the nursery, and makes a splendid breeding place for myriads of tiny frogs. Wide gravel paths surround the vast thuya-hedged plots, where rows of cuttings alternate with vegetables for the château. Red begonias grow beside the strawberry bed while white begonias border the lettuce patch – a combination of practicality and beauty learned from Villandry.

Having contemplated the serene, well-kept gardens, it is interesting to see the long and patient work which goes on behind the scenes. But all the work is justified by the results: too many parks and gardens in France have formal box parterres that have degenerated into a ghostly tracery of dead plants.

Just as the château's medieval past was preserved by the eighteenth-century transformations, so in the garden eighteenth-century formality combines happily with colourful and crowded Victorian abundance. Madame de Bastard has always given her time and energy unstintingly to the maintenance of Hautefort's perfection, and her courage and generosity have been responsible for the fine restoration of the château and the beauty of its gardens.

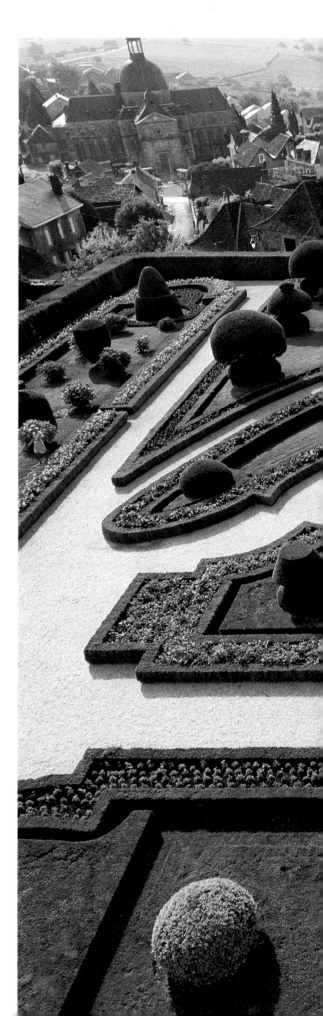

La Petite Rochelle

Le Perche
(La Comtesse Hélène d'Andlau)

A PAINTING is not judged by the size of the canvas, nor a literary work by its length – and we do not measure the beauty of a garden by its size. Yet space is a primary factor in laying out a garden, and Hélène d'Andlau was faced with the problem of a flat, disproportionately thin rectangle, about eighty yards by twenty-five, in which to design her garden in 1976.

She did find a few aces in her hand: a simple rustic house facing south, bordered to the east by an old wall, and a series of smaller buildings including an open-pillared barn to the west. At the bottom of the site two century-old walnut trees formed an arch framing a landscape of sky, hills and fields.

Her first task was to break the monotony of the rectangle by creating new levels: the ground was gently banked to form a grassy terrace in front of the house, above a low retaining wall laid parallel to the façade. The wall was double, with a hollow centre to be filled with earth and planted with helianthemum, *Œthionema grandiflora*, Hidcote lavender and other low plants. The ground behind it would be nearly invisible from the sitting room, accentuating the optical illusion of a gentle slope down to the walnut trees. A *Prunus* 'Amanogawa' grows on the sloping central lawn with a 'Nozomi' rose planted at its foot, encircling the trunk like a rosy ribbon in summer after the shell-pink cherry blossoms have faded. An amelanchier makes another focal point on the lawn nearer the house, its rich autumn colours rivalling the beauty of the fragrant white spring flowers. A wide, curving border flowers under the old wall.

Many planting experiments were possible in this enclosed, sunny and protected part of the garden, where the neutral pH factor and rich earth favour relatively fragile plants despite winter temperatures which can fall below −10° Centigrade in this part of Normandy. The temptation to grow camellias under the old wall was irresistible. *Camellia sasanqua* 'Papaver' and 'Rosea Plena' produce fragrant flowers when the winter is mild, and C. 'Salutation', 'Anticipation' and 'Adolphe Audusson' bloom each spring. A young *Ceanothus impressus* has already grown higher than the wall, and espaliered with the spring-flowering ceanothus 'Italian Skies' provides a harvest of blue in the garden. Two other ceanothus grow behind the walnut trees against another warm wall: summer-flowering *C. papillosus* and the dark blue *C. burkwoodii*. The same wall protects a large blue-flowering *Abutilon vitifolium* which blooms in May, a large shrub-like *Romneya coulteri*, Rosa *lævigata*, the 'Cherokee Rose', and another rose seldom seen so far north, 'La Follette'.

An unpainted wooden trellis against the house supports climbing roses 'Clair Matin', 'Charlotte Armstrong', 'Neige Rose' and the late Dutch honeysuckle *Lonicera periclymenum* 'Serotina'. A narrow border under the trellised wall is filled with spring- and autumn-flowering bulbs such as *Sternbergia lutea*, *Schizestylis coccinea*, belladonna lilies and a few other delicate plants, including *cistus* 'Silver Queen' and the lovely glossy leaved *Hebe bulkeana*, that bears large lavender-blue flowers in May and June.

The garden is divided into three different climatic zones: the warmest, in front of the house and to a lesser degree along the wall warmed by the setting sun, is thickly planted with clematis, *Kolkwitzia amabilis*, *Trachelospermum majus* and *Jasminium stephanense*. A second zone runs from the hollowed-out wall down to the walnut trees, where perennials including aquilegia, penstemon, erigeron, nepeta, hemerocallis and iris cluster around a few low-growing rhododendrons, among them the beautiful purple-flecked pink-flowering 'Tessa'. A sheltered rockery beneath the wall is planted with *Cistus skanbergii*, the pure white *C. monspeliensis* and Hélène d'Andlau's prized collection of daphne, including the rare *D. bholua* with sweetly scented winter flowers. Particular varieties have been selected to withstand the cold: *Daphne cneorum*, *D. burkwoodii* and *D. neapolitanum* are among her favourites. The rare pink-flowering perennial, rhodohypoxis, is protected in winter under raised panes of glass and cut ferns.

OPPOSITE A view towards
the new water garden,
through an opening
between the walnut trees.
ABOVE Climbing roses
and ceanothus encircle the
blue-painted shutters.

Beyond grow the cottage garden plants:
delphiniums, campanulas, herbaceous and tree
peonies, Japanese anemones, asters and phlox.
Among them are a few structural shrubs:
Deutzia 'Mont Rose' and *gracilis*, *Deutzia
elegantissima* 'Rosalind' and 'Fasciculata', *Cornus
florida* 'Cherokee Chief' and *Cornus kousa*, the
lilac-pink-flowering *Magnolia læbneri* 'Leonard
Messel' and *M. stellata*, and a *Prunus subhirtella*
'Autumnalis' with dainty white winter flowers.

A cooler shady zone begins near the great
walnut trees, perfect for rhododendrons,
azaleas, pieris, *Acer palmatum* and hydrangeas.
Particularly notable among the rhododendron
hybrids are 'Aladdin', 'Anita', 'Indomitable',
'Decorum' and 'Lady Berry'. Under the trees a
collection of rare bulbs flowers from early
spring through to autumn, together with various primulas, including variegated-leaved
lilies-of-the-valley and the rare, startling blue
'Brenenden', hardly ever seen in France. Later,
campanulas cast a blue haze, followed by the
fragile flowers of *Cyclamen neapolitanum* and
græcum.

Two principles determined the choice of
plants in the garden. The first aim was to obtain
almost permanent flowering by choosing a
wide variety of plants, many of which come
from England or the garden of Kerdalo in
Brittany (pp 132–7). The second was to impose
a severe selection of colour in this small space
where clashes would be glaringly obvious. The
bright yellow of forsythia and narcissus are
welcome after the grey of winter, but later
yellow is banished from the garden, except
perhaps for the dainty annual ground-cover
plant limnanthus, which seeds itself freely.
Everywhere blues and pinks reign unchallen-
ged, and enhanced by carefully placed silver
tones. Rare plants and aesthetic care have been
combined with skill to create a scene of sheer
delight.

No gardener's work is ever finished, and
there should always be room in the garden for
new arrivals. Beyond the walnut trees, around
a stone-bordered pond in an unused field, a
new plant world has recently emerged in just a
few brief months; and as the pink water-lilies
burst into flower, Hélène d'Andlau's new
gardening adventure begins.

Les Grandes Bruyères

Ingrannes, near Orléans

(Le Comte et la Comtesse de la Rochefoucauld)

THE NAME 'Les Grandes Bruyères', the great heathers, clearly tells us what to expect in this specialized garden. One grey winter's day in 1972, the Comte and Comtesse de la Rochefoucauld were returning home after a long walk in the forest around Orléans; struck by the beauty and intense colour of the heathers in flower, they decided then and there to use part of their land for the controlled cultivation of these plants. The first results on the sandy, slightly acid soil of the region were so encouraging that they soon found themselves hunting for heathers which would prolong the flowering season throughout the year.

As Bernard de la Rochefoucauld put it, 'I started out a complete novice, and in ten years I have found myself practically a heather specialist, having devoted most of my energies to this very accommodating plant.' The aim of the owners, once they started on the heather garden, was to assemble as complete a collection as possible of the 500 varieties in cultivation.

The garden would need only the minimum of maintenance, if any, once the ground-covering heathers were planted; and as heathers were to be the main feature, the unsophisticated, natural landscape of the forest border was preserved. Oaks, pines, birches and maples formed the backdrop for a broad lawn punctuated by curved beds of various shapes and sizes. These were then filled with heathers, together with hebe, cytisus, potentillas, pieris, magnolias, berberis, rhododendrons, specimen roses and conifers, to add height and variety of shape. In autumn, sedums and asters are a feature, but the low billowing waves of heather remain the stars of the garden.

Spring-flowering bulbs – mainly muscaris, white scillas and puschkinias – have naturalized themselves in the sandy soil. The wide paths are edged with slender tree trunks, lending a neat though informal touch to the beds of innumerable varieties of flowering heather: the native purple bell heather *Erica cinerea*, the tree heather *Erica arborea* 'Alpina', a ten-foot high tree covered with fragrant white flowers in spring, and a large variety of hybrid callunas. Winter-flowering heathers include *Erica darleyensis*, fat hummocks of *Erica carnea* and *Dabœcia cantabrica*, first found in Ireland on St Dabeoc's heath – hence the name heath for this group. Large colonies of *Dabœcia* have since been found growing wild in the south of France.

Contrary to popular belief, not all heathers need peat to flourish; any good kitchen garden-type soil suits many varieties, and *Erica carnea, arborea, vagans* and *darleyensis* easily survive traces of lime in the soil. Other varieties, for example the callunas and *Erica cinerea*, grow happily in poor sandy or acid soil.

Thus Bernard and Brigitte de la Rochefoucauld have become knowledgeable specialists and collectors, and their garden today is a showcase for several hundred varieties of heather. The range of colours is extraordinary – yellows, bronze, gold, white, violet, rose, amethyst and lavender – and a succession of flowers blooms season after season, thanks to careful rotation in the planting.

In a wooded area of roughly forty acres beyond the heather garden, Bernard de la Rochefoucauld has established a 'geographical' arboretum of trees, collected from all over the world but native to climates similar to that of Les Grandes Bruyères. The North American 'tulip tree', the *Liriodendron tulipifera*, liquidambars, scarlet-leaved oaks, *Magnolia acuminata*, the greenish-blue and yellow-metallic-leaved 'Cucumber tree', cornus, taxodiums, and long-lived elegant tsugas all grow here, together with a fine collection of conifers from the west coast of North America, including the majestic Californian redwood, *Sequoia sempervirens*, and the imposing calocedrus.

Superb trees from the Japanese island of Hokkaido, where curiously the climate is similar to that of Orléans, include the rare long-leaved Daimyo oak *Quercus dentata*, *Clerodendrum trichotomum* with its heavily scented summer-blooming white flowers, magnolias and cryptomerias.

The arboretum also boasts many maples with their glorious autumn foliage, pink-flowering albizias, and zelkova, a tree akin to the ill-fated elm. Particularly lovely are the birches, especially the beautiful *Betula albosinensis*, whose bark has a red and pink sheen, *B. septentrionalis* with glossy orange bark, and the western Chinese *B. platyphylla szechuanica*, with chalk-white bark. Many trees have been grown from seed, giving them a better chance to acclimatize. Once they have grown to full maturity, the arboretum will become an open-air schoolroom in which to study trees and their habits of growth.

A raised terrace garden near the house, overlooking the 'wild' landscape of natural planting, is traditionally laid out with box- and yew-edged squares filled with hebes and teucriums. The Chilean 'monkey flower', mimulus, spills over the urns bordering the paths. A rose- and clematis-covered pergola edged with lavender runs the length of the garden, dressed with a fine collection of old-fashioned roses: pale pink 'Duchesse de Montebello', 'Deep Crimson', 'Baron Girod de l'Ain', 'Cuisse de Nymphe Emue' (discreetly named 'Maiden's Blush' in English), violet-purple 'Reine des Violettes', 'Caroline Testout', the vigorous rambler 'Albertine', 'Léontine Gervais', salmon pink 'François Juranville', and deep pink 'Paul Neyron'.

But even the rich colours of roses and clematis cannot prevent your attention from returning to the heathers in their curved beds below, for their pastel shades are, after all, the keynote of Les Grandes Bruyères.

Château de Villandry

Joué-les-Tours, near Tours
(Monsieur et Madame Carvallo)

VILLANDRY is a remarkable negation of virtually every concept of gardening since the Renaissance. Not only does it scorn the achievements of French eighteenth-century gardens with Le Nôtre's endless vistas; it also totally ignores the English romantic tradition.

It is the most French of all gardens of France. Hugh Johnson aptly called it 'the ultimate kitchen garden', for it is an attempt to create beauty with fruit and vegetables. The surprising thing about it is that it was planned and laid out by a Spaniard in this century.

Joachim Carvallo was born in 1869 near the Portuguese border, where his father earned his living by pressing olives. An intelligent young man, he left for Madrid to study medicine, then travelled to Paris to study biology, intending to finish his education in Germany. But instead he remained in France to work on cinematography at the Institut Marey, and in Paris he met and married a young American medical student, Ann Colman. Looking for a place to settle in the country, they went to see the Château of Villandry, whose owner, a local pharmacist, planned to pull it down and sell the stones. The Carvallos bought the château and its land in 1906.

Situated a few miles west of Tours, Villandry is built in a small sheltered valley near a hillside facing the river Loire. The valley had been terraced to form the garden, which was closed off on one side by the village – an arrangement typical of medieval and Renaissance times, but later considered unacceptable.

The present château was begun in 1533 by Jean le Breton, François I's Secretary of State. The Marquis de Castellane bought the property in 1754 and attempted a *jardin à l'anglaise* on this unlikely site, filling in the moats to create

The sixteenth-century Château of Villandry rises behind its unique glory – the vast ornamental kitchen gardens.

OPPOSITE Box designs in
the *Jardin d'Amour*
symbolize four forms of
profane love: adulterous,
tragic, passionate and
tender.

ABOVE Wooden trellises
espaliered with apple and
pear trees frame each of
the nine square gardens in
the *potager*.

terraces and covering up the parterres. The château soon changed hands and even briefly fell into those of Napoleon's eldest brother, Joseph Bonaparte. For most of the nineteenth century it belonged to a banking family, the Hainguerlos, whose staggering lack of taste was responsible for some disastrous architectural additions to the façade.

Terrified by the responsibility he had assumed, Dr Carvallo began nevertheless to restore the château to its original simplicity, gradually correcting the ravages of time and poor ownership. In the park, the east terrace, retaining wall and eighteenth-century canals and lake were uncovered and the moats cleared; thus the garden plan began to develop, using the eighteenth-century canals and terraces as the main axis upon which to balance the layout. Once a scientist of liberal convictions, Dr Carvallo now came to believe in the medieval theory that beauty was the natural outcome of a fixed and hierarchical social order based on religion. 'Our ancestors had a very different concept of life', he wrote:

the house was built to last, and to answer all the needs of the family, and around it, but on a lower level, were clustered the outbuildings. The château itself was a closed courtyard, and behind it stretched terraced gardens. Thus each element of the domestic order had its place, strictly ordered and with no possible confusion: the animals were lower than the servants, who were subordinate to their masters. This hierarchy in the house was also to be observed in the gardens. According to its importance, the house had one or many gardens: a kitchen garden, an ornamental garden and a water garden ... Of these, the kitchen garden was

placed below the house, on the same level as the stables, which provided manure. The ornamental garden, on a higher level, adjoined the house and formed an open-air salon; and finally the water garden was located on high ground, where springs surfaced.

The first ornamental garden, the *Jardin d'Amour*, was begun before 1914, and stretches south behind the salon windows on the ground floor of the château. Four squares symbolize four forms of love, with a selection of annuals giving the dominant colour to each square. Yellow flowers bloom between patterns of fans and love letters, to symbolize the frivolity of adulterous love, while red – the colour of blood – fills the square of tragic love, with its whirlpool of swords and daggers. *Amour tendre* alternates hearts with flames outlined in orange, while the northern square represents passionate love, *l'amour folle*, with a strange maze of broken hearts.

The *jardin d'ornement* continues on the other side of the moat, its green tapestry of mixed box forming a page of calligraphy from a Moorish manuscript when seen from a higher terrace. Iris, lavender, santolina and other perennials silver the empty spaces.

But the great glory and unique feature of Villandry is the kitchen garden. Here Dr Carvallo drew his inspiration from the engravings made by Jacques Androuet de Cerceau (1515–84) published in two volumes as *Les Plus Excellents Bastiments de France*. He became convinced that de Cerceau's ornamental gardens were in fact kitchen gardens, and this reinforced his belief that the ideal garden was the closed medieval monastic garden with its culinary and medicinal herbs and vegetables

and occasional flowers grown for the altar.

The kitchen garden at Villandry covers an acre, divided into nine squares, each with its own geometrical patterns. The beds are separated by shining paths of *mignonnette* sand from the Loire. Cordons of pear and apple trees grow along the low wooden trellises – grey tinged with soft blue by copper sulphate treatments – and more wooden trellises with semi-circular arbours shrouded in climbing roses mark the intersections of the paths. Without seeing Villandry it would be hard to imagine that the shapes and colours of vegetables could create such harmony: neat sword-like leeks, feathery-leaved carrots, the purple and green heads of cabbages, exotic looking artichokes and the golden-green sheaths of corn, all neatly framed in box edgings. Clipped pyramids of pear trees stand guard near red rose trees, red being the colour of sacred love, and the rose tree a traditional symbol of the gardener-monk. Strawberries are bedded next to white-leaved cabbages, and rosy apples ripen among the pink petunias. Madame Carvallo, the wife of Dr Carvallo's grandson, traces the two-yearly planting schemes in coloured pencil on huge sheets of paper, establishing the desired effect for the coming seasons. She avoids combining the same shades of green, and corrects what she considers past mistakes – for instance planting tomatoes next to sweet peppers, not because the reds clashed, but because of the similarity of the greens.

Every plant is grown from seed ordered mainly in France. 30,000 plants are grown in the traditional way in hot beds, made from a mixture of horse manure and dead leaves from the thousand lime trees that form Villandry's pleached avenues. The first plants are bedded out in April and follow a generally blue and yellow scheme; the second wave of vegetables and flowers replaces them in June, to be lifted at the first frost, about November. In summer and autumn stronger colours predominate: reds, pinks and orange mingled with the yellow of ripening apples and pears. As the vegetables ripen they are picked for family use, and the excess is left in large baskets for visitors.

Apart from all this there are twenty miles of box edging to be cut in April, 160 topiary yews to be clipped, and the lime trees to pleach, on top of the daily maintenance of the paths and plants. All this is done by four gardeners, working by hand and using the traditional methods espoused by Dr Carvallo. No weed-killers or electrical equipment are allowed at Villandry. The plants in the kitchen garden are rotated every third year and a top-dressing of cow manure is dug in every autumn.

On the village side of the top terrace Madame Carvallo is making a new garden of forty herbs, planted in the existing pattern of circles crossed by topiary yews. This follows firmly the traditions of old Dr Carvallo, who wanted to make a definitive break from the too-natural English garden, and wrote: 'Unnatural as this wonderful formal garden is to English eyes, it is to that degree more human'.

Certainly, large as it is, Villandry's scale is perfectly adjusted to human capacities. There are no daunting Baroque vistas, for it is designed to meet human needs – the growing of vegetables, the enjoyment of flowers, walking in the sun or shade – and all set in a framework of an intellectual rather than emotional aesthetic. As Dr Carvallo once justly remarked, 'God loves Villandry'.

Semicircular wooden arbours covered with climbing roses mark the intersection of the paths.

OVERLEAF RIGHT The astonishing harmony of vegetables and flowers. OVERLEAF LEFT Standard red roses, a symbol for the gardener-monks, rise above red-stalked rhubarb.

Jas Créma

Le Barroux, near Carpentras, Haute-Provence
(La Baronne de Waldner)

NOT many people have the courage to leave a garden that they have laid out and brought to perfection over thirty years in order to start a new garden in an unfamiliar landscape and an alien climate. The Baroness de Waldner was forced to leave her marvellous garden at Mortefontaine in the Ile de France near Paris when, to her surprise, the lease on her house, La Grange, was not renewed.

Having searched in vain for a new place in Normandy, her first choice, she left Paris to stay with friends in Haute-Provence, where, out driving one day, she saw by chance the perfect house: a severely beautiful eighteenth-century *bastide* built on a low hill facing the old hill-town of Le Barroux, with its restored Renaissance fairy-tale château. Jas Créma is set between the lacy mountains of Montmirail and the plain of Carpentras, with a sublime view of the beautiful snow-capped Mont Ventoux. Captivated by the breath-taking beauty of the site, and also by the challenge of creating an entirely new type of garden in unfamiliar conditions, the Baroness claims that she was able to envisage the main plan for the garden at first sight. The gravelled drive from the bottom of the hill to the front of the house would have to go, the huge chestnut blocking the façade of the house would be cut down and a series of descending terraces cut out of the hill leading down from the house. The problems, however, were manifold: first and foremost, the house was not for sale. With enormous persistence, the Baroness persuaded the owner, a widow who lived alone in the large house, to sell, and the transfer was signed on 10 July 1979. Then she realized she had never asked about the water supply – and a plentiful permanent supply of water is essential if you want a garden in this sun-baked arid part of France. Lulu de Waldner went straight to the Mayor of Le Barroux, who assured her that the property was dry. She went higher up, to the Prefect of the region, asking him to have the old records checked, hoping for a mention of a vanished spring or well. Everyone in the district denied any such possibility. Undeterred, but by this time extremely perturbed, she brought in a local water-diviner. He walked around with his rod under the anxious scrutiny of Madame de Waldner, dug a hundred yards down and found nothing. At the beginning of the following year, well after the work of restoration and ground-levelling had started, with lorry-loads of plants already arriving from her Mortefontaine garden, she brought in someone else, again with no luck. Then, miraculously, a large supply of water was finally discovered. It was a day for celebration. The garden could go ahead.

The soil was poor, so new earth was brought in, excavated from the site of a future factory. But the first priority was a greenhouse to shelter the plants sent down from La Grange, for these tender greenhouse specialities were grouped outdoors around the fountain and winter was approaching. The architect Alexander Fabre, following Lulu de Waldner's instructions to the letter, for she knew exactly what she needed and wanted, built what is probably the first really modern private greenhouse in France. The result is a total success, as well as a visual delight both inside and out, particularly because it houses a beautiful collection of very decorative passion flowers. There are about 500 known species of passiflora, all but a few too tender to be grown outdoors.

The greenhouse is built against the outer

The hill-town and Renaissance château of Le Barroux rise behind the characteristic line of cypress trees that edges the lavender field at the end of the garden. The punctuating arches are covered in *Banksiae* roses.

wall of a barrel-vaulted room once used for
storage, which has now been made into a
charming sitting room and study. It is separated from the greenhouse by a sealed glass
door, made to a romantic Gothic design by the
local blacksmith, and the arrangement gives
the impression of a winter garden opening on
to the sitting room. Another similar door
opens on to a secret enclosed herb garden in
front of the greenhouse, with a distant view of
the violet-blue snow-capped Mont Ventoux
over the wall. A border of black irises lines the
greenhouse terrace, fronted with lemon trees
and jasmine in terracotta pots. A stone owl
perches on the wall behind a bed of Lulu de
Waldner's favourite miniature roses, grown as
shrubs and standards. Miniature roses often
seem lost in a large garden, but here they are
perfect; the most enchanting are 'Mr Bluebird',
the glowing 'Pink Rose' and the aptly named
'White Gem'. Nearby is an interesting shrub,

the charming round rose-flowering *Raphiolepsis delacoursii*, and other special Waldner
touches are the ivy- and cactus-covered topiary
elephant and two topiary horses' heads of
clipped jasmine.

The lower part of the garden, with its baby
nectarine trees in nine box-bordered squares,
could be taken from a medieval painting. A
profusion of herbs grows beneath the nectarines: a mixture of mints, including the red-
stemmed *Mentha × gentilis*, thyme and tarragon.
Jasmine nightshade, *Solanum jasminoides*, covers
the wall, its ravishing pale blue flowers mingling with the bright pink blooms of 'Pink
Perpétue', an excellent, vigorous and recurrent
rose, particularly good in autumn when most
climbers bloom less profusely. Lulu de
Waldner grows her favourite pink camellias
under the wall, out of the glaring sun.

This part of Haute-Provence is unique in its
stark uncompromising beauty: the light is

strong and pure, winters are harsh, snow often turns the countryside white in late December, and the winds are cutting. In summer the sun is pitiless, and shade and water are scarce. There could be no greater contrast with the romantic woods and misty light of the Ile de France around Mortefontaine. Taking all this into account, the plan of the garden had to be strong and bold, composed of large, well-defined spaces. The long straight terraces would have simple, undecorated stone walls to divide the garden from the rolling vineyards and low rocky hills. Geometric shapes – rectangles, squares and circles – would be used, and vague, meandering or blurred lines avoided. Her much-loved roses, foliage plants and flowering perennials would be secondary details, held within strong architectural lines. The two main borders, one under the high top wall, the other following the wall on the right-hand side of the garden, would provide ample space both for favourite plants brought from La Grange and for growing and observing new plants.

The garden is all the more fascinating and instructive because it is young and still developing. The main architectural plan takes precedence over the inventive and charming touches to be found throughout the garden, and these details at the same time soften the bold lines. Viewed from the terrace in front of the house or from an upper window, the plan is brilliantly clear. Two long terraces cut out of the hillside lead down to a large flat field of lavender, bordered by a long line of cypresses. The terraces are bisected by a straight main avenue bordered with oleanders, and the three levels are connected by stone steps, while the twin Gothic gates provide a touch of romantic fantasy. They are painted the lovely *bleu de Versailles* used for the ironwork throughout the gardens, which was all made by the local blacksmith from Le Barroux. Large hedged squares break up the two terraces, seven on the lower, five on the higher, and all but one topped with high central 'vases' of clipped pittosporum (the right-hand upper square was left vaseless to avoid the trap of banal repetition). All are planted individually, with hebe, silver-leaved *Senecio maritima*, pinks or oxalis.

Beyond the blue gate is the flat lower garden, with paths radiating from a circle; they are of unequal length, shorter towards the house, longer towards the line of cypresses bordering the property, and some end in further small circles. Before the paths were laid a white powder was used to trace them on the ground – an excellent idea, as the design was easily seen from the house, and was simple to change. The focal point of the garden is the enormous topiary elephant in the central square. The blacksmith made the frame, designed of course by Madame de Waldner, who planted wild box to cover it, just as she made topiary swans at La Grange; the box grew beautifully for two months, then died a natural death. Desperate, she planted *Banksiæ* roses to cover the hideously naked structure, and was astonished to discover that they could be beautifully pruned and trained into any shape. Now the elephant is a spectacular sight, covered each spring with thousands of yellow roses and a splendid green the rest of the year. Why an elephant? Lulu de Waldner seems equally puzzled, and answers perhaps because Hannibal crossed the not too distant Alps on elephant back, or perhaps as a reminder of her beloved India. The rest of the field is planted with row upon row of lavender, giving a marvellous *pointilliste* effect from above and a delightfully fragrant cloud of blue and green from below. At the same time, it provides a perfect bridge between the cultivated plants growing on the terraced gardens and the wild landscape of Haute-Provence.

Irises grow wild in Provence, and they were the only plants Madame de Waldner found growing at Jas Créma. The hill behind the house is carpeted with blue irises right up to the higher vineyards. Great clumps of them were seeded and divided along the lower slopes, and huge new beds of bearded irises were planted behind the garden wall near the mulberry. Irises encircle the fig tree at the end of the wall, and further down there are yet more: a stunning mixture of brown and blue.

The gardens are filled with unforgettable cameos: the silvery-lilac rose, 'Blue Moon', flowering between the lavender-blue spikes of acanthus beside a group of agapanthus; passion flowers covering the wall behind a ravishing pale shell-pink centifolia 'Fantin Latour', the favourite rose of Flemish painters in the seventeenth century; a small high rectangle in the

A huge elephant, covered each spring with yellow *Banksiae* roses, is the focal point in the field of lavender.

OPPOSITE LEFT Baroness de Waldner designed the greenhouse as an extension of the *bastide* for her collection of passion flowers.

OPPOSITE RIGHT The architectural design of the 'young' garden seen from the house.

One white tulip in a bed of violets against the massive trunk of the plane tree in front of the *bastide*.

corner of two walls, planted thick with old-fashioned pinks and tiny rock-garden succulents; prostrate ceanothus used as ground cover – the list is endless.

Some trees were incorporated into the plan of the garden. The cypress that once stood at the top of the old entrance drive marks the upper right-hand corner, while lower down the wall was built with an opening to accommodate an old mulberry tree. Two fig trees grow on the side of the house near a newly planted weeping cherry and another shades the end of the wall. Dappled light falls through the leaves of a huge plane tree on the paved terrace in front of the house. All the trees are ringed with large smooth pebbles and charmingly underplanted with wild violets and other small plants. Cherry trees line the rosemary-bordered path on the site of the old drive, between the wall and the vineyards that surround the property, and rows of cherries grow among the vines. Tall palm-like dracænas grow against the simple bare façade of the *bastide*, a very unusual and effective way of dressing a wall.

A raised swimming pool with pool-house and terrace was built above the high rose-covered retaining wall in the end corner of the gardens, below which three cool-frames brought from La Grange are filled with Madame de Waldner's favourite pelargoniums, pinks and poppies. A cutting garden of roses, grown for the house, lies just below the cool-frames. The Baroness is famous for her ravishing tiny flower arrangements and marvellous bouquets. Particularly oustanding are the coral-pink 'Blessings', amber-coloured 'Apricot Nectar' and deeper 'Just Joey' and the brown-pink 'Café' and 'Brownie'. The pool terrace is a study in yellow and white: pots of lemon trees line the white walls covered with the excellent yellow rose 'Mermaid', and the terrace is lined with box grown as small standard trees, their heads clipped into round balls. Three topiary horses' heads end the terrace, in front of a sweeping view over the countryside to Mont Ventoux, with the gardens and the silhouette of the château-topped town in the foreground.

Baroness de Waldner has a special giant parasol that she uses to shade anything she transplants from the summer sun; this little detail is indicative of the care and love she gives to every plant in her garden, as is the fact that Jas Créma's greenhouse was finished long before the house. Jas Créma means 'burnt sheepfold' in Old Provençal – a charming name, now strangely inappropriate for this phoenix of a garden under Mont Ventoux.

Le Pigeonnier Saint-Jean

near Grasse, Alpes-Maritimes
(Mr and Mrs Schlienger)

LE PIGEONNIER SAINT-JEAN is a simple but lovely old *bastide* surrounded by a garden of infinite charm and poetry. The story of its acquisition is as romantic as the property itself. The farm was bought before the Second World War by an American lady, Miss Hodges, the daughter of one of J.P. Morgan's partners, to protect the view below her villa. Meanwhile, the present owner, Mr Hubert Schlienger, the head of a family perfume business in Grasse, saw the house, fell in love with it and determined to buy it. For almost twenty years he ceremoniously called on Miss Hodges to persuade her to sell him the property. Over their yearly cup of tea she delighted in refusing all offers on the grounds that, firstly, he was a bachelor, a state she profoundly disapproved of, and, secondly, that he was French. She

A lovely distant view of the old town of Grasse beyond two of the old stone retaining walls that form the series of terraced *planches*. The lower wall is covered with self-seeding pink valerian.

could not approve of Frenchmen, as their traditional pastime was defrauding their government. When he came to tea in 1960, he brought with him the lady he had waited for and loved as long as he had coveted the Pigeonnier Saint-Jean. The next day he received an imperative summons from Miss Hodges, who announced that as he was about to remove her first objection to the sale, and in such a satisfactory way, she would overlook his nationality.

Until 1962 the property was a real farm. The ground floor of the house lodged the livestock while the farmer and his family lived on the upper floors. The land was used to grow jasmine for the Grasse perfume industry and was treeless save for a few old cypresses. The garden only began to take shape after the house was restored, and it grew at its own natural rhythm around the house and along the terraces, or *planches* as they are called in the south of France. All the existing, natural elements – the olive trees, cypresses, old stone walls and central downhill path – were retained and incorporated in the garden by the Schliengers,

aided by the excellent M. Calabre, gardener at Le Pigeonnier since the beginning.

The property can hardly be seen from the road above, and it is almost impossible to imagine the charm and peace below until you walk under its narrow green archway formed by two huge cypresses. This leads to the front of the house, which is joined at right angles to the smaller, tiled *pigeonnier*. The extraordinarily vigorous rose 'La Follette' climbs in and out of the cypresses, its lovely, double rose-pink and creamy copper flowers set off wonderfully by the dark green of its host. This prolific rose bears over 2,000 flowers annually and is at its best in the warm climate of the south of France; raised by Lord Brougham's gardener at Cannes, it will grow well on any sunny, sheltered wall. 'La Follette' shares its space with the beautiful Banksian rose *Banksiæ lutescens*, the Chinese rambler happily rediscovered at Sir Thomas Hanbury's famous vanished garden La Mortola at Menton. Over 50,000 small yellow fragrant flowers are produced on long, arching tresses every year in April and May.

A stone bench bordered with rounded,

ABOVE Irises grow wild in the old olive orchard on the hillside.

RIGHT Irises grow through euphorbia and rosemary around a small stone fountain tucked in a corner near the house.

OPPOSITE Climbing 'Madame Meilland' ('Peace' in England) grows up the pale apricot walls of the *bastide*, above the heavily-planted arched pergola.

clipped box stands against the façade of the *pigeonnier*, and more clipped box is mixed with flowers planted in front of the long stone balustrade that overlooks the marvellous view of the wide and fertile valley below Grasse. In the nineteenth century the valley stretching down from Grasse towards the sea was filled with a solid mass of roses grown for the perfume industry. Now, alas, the basic ingredients of perfume are mainly chemical – the few essential oils still used are imported from countries with cheap labour – and the roses have long since given way to housing. But the view is only part of the delight, for there is also the satisfying simplicity of this traditional house, with its pale apricot walls, grey-blue wooden shutters, and the pergola that runs the length of the building. A tangled mixture of grape vines, jasmine and honeysuckle festoons the pergola, and their green shade shelters a lovely disorder of flowering gardenias, white azaleas, scented geraniums, abutilons and a few annuals, all in terracotta pots, large and small. Climbing 'Madame Meilland', symbolically named 'Peace' when it was smuggled out of

Two cypresses covered with the rampant rose 'La Follette' form an arched entrance in the angle between the *bastide* and its smaller *pigeonnier*.

France during the war as a seedling and now known throughout the world by that name, covers the façade of the house, growing right up to the white-framed windows. Although 'Madame Meilland', with over-large flowers, is often, if not always, too vigorous for a small garden, here the enormous yellow flushed-pink flowers are perfect against the grey-tinged apricot of the wall.

The *bastide*, the smaller *pigeonnier* and the long stone balustrade form three sides of a grassed rectangle. The fourth side is bordered with a mass of tree peonies near a small, quiet fountain. Yellow and white irises and euphorbias growing through rosemary surround a stone trough, thickly planted with pansies.

The garden continues past the pergola and the top of the cypress-lined central path and narrows into a deep, curving ribbon of grass beside a high stone wall that ends by a tall cypress. The wall is underplanted with a variety of iberis, a pink-flowering shrub rose, a rounded bed of bearded irises, and

a few erect hollyhocks. Glossy arum lilies are tucked into a corner of the wall and pink valerian grows through the cracks – a recurrent theme throughout the garden, softening almost all of the many walls. In the left border, a pittosporum grows through an olive tree, while the huge white flowers of the tree peonies catch the light and shine against soft silver-leaved plants and a few dark purple foxgloves. The garden continues above the wall, up a grassy path set with stone steps to a lawn adjoining the side of the house. Big pots of scented pink geraniums are set among clumps of tall daisies near the side door. There is a silver, purple and blue border of mixed aubretia, lavender, veronicas, blue aquilegia, and violets set in the shade. The garden is separated from the open fields beyond by a group of mauve and purple lilacs, pale lavender-blue bearded irises and deep pockets of blue pansies and lavender. In the open fields there is a ravishing mixture of naturalized irises growing wild under olive trees.

The lower terraces are invisible from the house, marked only by a line of dark cypresses along the descending path which, like the lower terraces, appears to exist outside time and without formal invention – it seems just a happy coincidence that a few cunningly placed pale apricot irises echo the colour of the house glimpsed above the path. Lilacs grow among the cypresses and the path is bordered with euphorbias, rosemary and bergenia. The wonderful visual effect created by a blanket of self-seeding valerian growing through every crack in a lower wall also seems accidental. Beyond this pink cloud there is a breath-taking side view of the old town of Grasse. All the terrace walls are used as partly wild gardens. One base wall is thickly covered with Meilland's strident crimson rose 'Cocktail', with bright yellow stamens, the strong pink 'Princess Margaret' and the apricot-pink climbing 'Gruss an Aachen'. Valerian grows everywhere on the back wall of the pool terrace, through the climbing 'Madame Meilland', more 'Princess Margaret' and the deep velvet-red, wonderfully fragrant 'Etoile de Hollande'. A low stone wall has been added to form a knee-high bed against the higher wall, and is planted with a tangle of nasturtiums, geraniums, verbena and other bright annuals.

A lovely detail in the garden is the rose hedge which separates the pool lawn from the path. Five lovely hybrid musk 'Penelopes' were trained to form this balustrade covered with clusters of pale apricot-salmon flowers, a wonderful idea for a garden. Too often hybrid musks are lamentably absent from gardens where they could be used grouped in tall borders and as hedges.

A deep mixed border of arums, antirrhinums, pink and white dianthus and pale-blue-flowering nepeta grow under the slightly sloping wall on the other side of the path. In the back part of this border, orange-flowering abutilons nod towards the ever-present pink and white valerian and climbing roses. There is a grove of lemon trees stretching away on one of the lower levels, while another narrow terrace serves as a simple kitchen garden, brightened by clumps of phlox.

The bottom terrace is a semicircular orchard of olive and cherry trees. One ancient fig tree stands in the middle of the owners' favourite part of the garden, where the warm peace of the Midi is most deeply felt.

Charles de Noailles, owner of the nearby Villa Noailles (pp 202–11), loved to drop in on Le Pigeonnier Saint-Jean for a glass of *vin d'oranges* and a stroll through the garden. He never imposed his ideas nor made suggestions, but always brought a special cutting from his own garden or a plant from his travels, and would nod with pleasure and contentment over the development of this totally charming and unpretentious garden. The owners freely admit that their approach to gardening is instinctive, and that sometimes they do not know the name of a rose or the variety of a plant, but that they chose them for their beauty. And when you look across the curving 'Penelopes' covered with blushing roses under the flowering almond tree and past the line of cypresses towards the gentle hills, the violet and blue background of the garden, you know that here charm and quiet are all that matters.

An iron railing and steep steps lead to the high garden above the heavily-planted stone wall.

Château de la Garoupe

Cap d'Antibes, Alpes-Maritimes
(Mr Anthony Norman)

THE CHATEAU DE LA GAROUPE and its gardens occupy the entire eastern end of the Cap d'Antibes. At the end of the last century Lady Aberconway of Bodnant, north Wales, visited the Côte d'Azur and fell in love with its wild beauty. Excited by the possibilities of a Mediterranean garden, she persuaded her husband to buy the entire Cap d'Antibes.

The huge white Italianate château was finished in 1905, south-facing and overlooking the sea. The gardens, designed by Lady Aberconway, were laid out by 1907. Both the house and the front gardens are very much in the grand Edwardian manner, in keeping with the exceptional site. The magnificent view to the south, a vast expanse of sea and rocky coastline, together with the equally exceptional northern view, encompassing the entire Bay of Nice and the high Alps beyond, determined the size of the château and the scale of the main gardens. Lady Aberconway matched natural beauty to grandeur and elegance, and used her botanical experience to fill the gardens with treasures, rare plants blending perfectly into the natural landscape of the Provençal *garrigue*.

The château looks out on to the large and elegant main terrace; Italian vases punctuate the symmetry of the formal gardens, two vast carpets of grey and green. Below, two smaller terraces lead to a broad and imposing flight of white marble steps descending towards the sea.

The Second World War marked a cæsura between Lady Aberconway's designs and the transformations about to be undertaken by her grandson, Mr Anthony Norman. Before the end of hostilities he managed to take a brief leave of absence from his military duties and flew into Nice only days after the Germans had withdrawn. Conditions at La Garoupe were not too bad, as the Swiss head gardener had been able to continue his work during the German occupation. However, the Germans, fearing an Allied landing on the Côte d'Azur, had planted over 2,000 landmines on the property. Ironically, German efficiency saved the situation: their careful plans of the minefields, sent to Berlin, were miraculously discovered by Mr Norman. German prisoners were pressed into service to clear them, and the ammonium nitrate from the mines was used as dressing for the orange trees on the terrace. The only evidence left of the German presence is the bathing hut built on the edge of the rocks.

Thus the end of the war marked the beginning of the transformation Mr Norman brought about at La Garoupe; a thoughtful, slow process, always showing respect for the designs and intentions of his remarkable grandmother. For example, the main entrance had been grassed, and groups of cypresses towered over the lawn near the central flower beds. Grass rarely grows well in the south of France and Lady Aberconway never achieved the hoped-for perfection of an English lawn, nor were the central beds in proportion with the grandeur of the view. Some ten years ago Mr Norman, inspired by the design of the Piazza del Popolo in Rome with its two vast semicircles, designed the two geometric carpets that cover the first terraces. He wanted a circular design, formal in the middle, and so added box pyramids in circles, also of box. Having experimented with two different lavenders, he arrived finally at the present arrangement, a perfect combination of rosemary, santolina and *Lavandula pinnata*, all clipped twice yearly to a neat, even height. The vastness of the design and its elegant tranquillity are a perfect foil to

The main terrace, carpeted in green and grey. Broad white marble steps bordered by slender cypress trees lead down to the Mediterranean.

BELOW Lemon trees and daturas line the sheltered walls of the pergola. RIGHT An astrolabe in the centre of four clipped orange trees in Mr Norman's *jardin de curé*.

the grandiose view of sky and sea.

Before the war, the balustrade in front of the château was lined with an oleander hedge. Now, orange trees edge the terrace, while tropical lotus, flowering white or pink in summer, fill large terracotta pots between the trees. Some six years ago Mr Norman created a massed border beneath the balustrade, after thickly planting the walls of the south façade with *Rosa banksiæ* and bougainvillea. On each side of the marble patio are striking clumps of *Echium candicans*, with towering deep blue spires, superb plants suitable only for the mildest regions. A rare and special shrub to the left of the balustrade is *Grayia polygaloides*, with Chinese red filaments, a present from *Les Parcs et Jardins de France* in appreciation of Mr Norman's unfailing courtesy and generosity in allowing special visitors into his gardens. All the standard roses that bloom in the border are from the local Meilland nurseries: the deep blood-red 'Léopold Senghor', the lovely 'Catherine Deneuve' and 'Clair Matin'. Another delight is the night-blooming jasmine

Cestrum nocturnum, and daturas, growing happily in the full sun. They are well watered, and provide what Mr Norman considers 'the secret of a garden ... plenty of white'. Tangerine-coloured oleanders are grown as standards among clusters of *Abutilon* 'Royal Scarlet' and a collection of hibiscus. Other shrubs include the scarlet-flowering *Punica granatum*, buddleias and sophoras.

The two lower terraces echo the density and variety of planting in the château border. The second terrace is bordered by dark blue lithospermum and holds impressive groups of tall yuccas among cerise- and cream-flowering cytisus. The yellow-green *Robinia* 'Frisia' contrasts beautifully with the dark and stately cypresses. These two lower borders are the May gardens of La Garoupe, their beds filled with sun-loving plants. Two magnificent *Magnolia grandiflora* grow on the lowest half-moon terrace, near the large Japanese cherries and the thornless honey locust, *Gleditsia* 'Sunburst'. And here the rose acacia, *Robinia hispida*, with its long racemes of deep rose flowers, makes a striking display with a fine variety of flowering shrubs: abelias, spiræa, weigelas and forsythias. Agapanthus line the front of the border, and groups of irises, planted in pockets amongst the trees and shrubs, continue the colour scheme against the glistening paperwhite *Romneya coulteri*.

From here broad marble steps descend to the

sea, flanked by an avenue of cypresses, pruned to an elegant pencil-thinness, with cone-shaped pittosporums marking each step. The avenue is edged with an outstanding collection of rock plants and the true sun-loving succulents: rosette-shaped aloes and handsome long-leaved yuccas, including *Yucca gloriosa* 'Nobilis' with marvellous sword-like leaves and spectacular red bell-shaped panicles. Summer brings the bright flowers of the pink belladonna lily, planted in groups between the grey and silver-green succulents.

The lower part of the garden is in a wilder vein. A low hedge of pittosporum marks a division between the marble steps and a natural planting of rosemary, myrtles and cytisus. A wide balcony overlooks the sea and the rocky coastline, which displays a varied profusion of plants: the low silver-leaved *Convolvulus cneorum*, covered with pink buds which open with the sun into shining white flowers from spring to autumn, *Coronila emerus*, the scorpion senna, lithospermum, and the dense downy-grey moon trefoil, *Medicago arborea*. The daisy-shaped colourful flowers of mesembryanthemum, which also only open in the full sun, clamber over the rocks.

Towards the point of the Cap, the gardens slowly fade into the wild *garrigue*. (The *garrigue* is not at all the same thing as the *maquis*; the latter indicates an acid soil, while the former is the arid chalk country typical of the Mediterranean.) A narrow avenue of cypresses leads from the formal parterre of the main terrace to a summer-house. On either side of the avenue large flowering rock roses have either replaced or intermingled with their wilder sisters. Umbrella pines add their familiar shape to the dense planting of brooms and bushy, woolly-shooted halimocistus. This typical landscape follows subtly upon the formal artifice of the gardens. Somehow the sun feels hotter here and the air is fragrant with a wild sweetness.

At the other end of the château, daturas crowd the pergola leading to the pool terrace, grown in large terracotta pots as small trees; the orange and pink trumpets of the Peruvian *Datura sanguinea* are particularly breathtaking. Lemon trees line the sheltered wall near the golden yellow-flowering *Datura chlorantha*, sharing space with the golden solandra and

Solanum crispa. The arches are festooned with tender climbers – scarlet and orange-flowering campsis, jasmine, wisteria, and the white *Clematis armandii* – all mingling with colourful trailing pelargoniums and roses.

The pergola ends with a small covered salon in an Oriental mood, with deep couches set against a bold design of blue and white tiles. Here you can relax in shaded comfort, looking back towards the open arches, with their display of flowering shrubs and climbers leading to the mixed borders of the pool, set in an emerald green lawn. The spirit of the pool terrace is English, although the dominant colours are the hot deep pinks and reds of the massed regal and zonal pelargoniums. Clumps of arum lilies and low-growing *Chrysanthemum frutescens* provide a creamy-white foil for them: the touches of white that make a garden.

Anthony Norman made a new level for the pool terrace, raising the surrounding ground to the same level as the pergola, and leaving the

The Italianate château from the lower terraces.

lawn on a slightly lower level. A row of exotic mandarins and kumquats marks the formal boundary between this and the two smaller gardens below. Here, there are three large *Lagerstræmia indica*, the lovely crêpe myrtle, with bark of mottled grey, pink and cinnamon and ravishing lilac-pink flowers. A small weeping *Pyrus salicifolia* and an old olive tree wreathed with a climbing philodendron add a cool touch of silver to the border. The Chinese *Buddleia fallowiana* attracts butterflies to its lilac-blue spikes, while hibiscus gives yet more colour to this glowing garden. Oleanders are grown as standards – 'much prettier', maintains Mr Norman.

Three steps lead down from these massed pinks, reds and violets into the secret white garden, seen ideally through the spray of the small central fountain. The garden is curtained off from the majestic view, as well as from the surrounding exuberant colours, by a circle of orange trees, underplanted with great clumps of white hydrangeas: 'Snowcap' and *H. paniculata grandiflora*. The green and white colour scheme is continued by white lilacs, 'Madame Lemoine', and lemon-scented philadelphus. Old oil jars, set on the tiny lawn, are filled to overflowing with chlorophytum, its variegated green and white striped leaves hung with white star-shaped flowers; and the white-edged *Euonymus* 'Silver Queen' makes a low outer hedge. This is a garden of green shade after the glaring sun, where the quiet sound of falling water inspires peace, and where the shaded white

OPPOSITE The white garden is a cool contrast to the rest of this Mediterranean garden.
ABOVE A vast design of clipped lavender and rosemary combined with santolina forms a perfectly proportioned carpet on the main terrace.

OPPOSITE ABOVE
Cypresses, pittosporums
and sun-loving succulents
line the steps down to the
rocky shore.
OPPOSITE BELOW This
almond tree in the centre
of the main avenue in the
spring garden is the oldest
tree in the region.

tones are as soft as moonlight.

Adjacent to the white garden and parallel to the pergola lies a small, square *jardin de curé*. Four rectangular beds, their inner sides curved to encircle an astrolabe, hold four formally clipped orange trees, underplanted with small studies in pink, white and orange.

The north garden is in total contrast to the formal south. The view, also spectacular, is very different: from this side the Mediterranean is enclosed in the graceful curves of the Bay of Nice, with the city mistily indistinct under the violet-blue high Alps. A flight of marble steps tempts you down a hill of flowering mimosas and groves of orange and olive trees. The steps are flanked by two large groups of shining green cycads, male plants on the left, females on the right, and bordered with the rosemary-leaved lithospermum, the stately agave-like rosetted Mexican plants *Beschorneria*, and the towering white foxtails of *Urginea maritima*.

At the bottom of the steps are the orange and olive groves. Some of the olive trees are over a thousand years old and are believed to have been planted by the Romans; but the most awesome and moving sight in the garden is an ancient almond tree, its ten-foot girth carefully supported with props placed under its branches. Known to be the oldest living tree in the region, it is a mysterious relic of ancient times. It stands in the middle of the broad main avenue, the focal point of the garden.

The loveliest walks in the northern spring garden are along the olive avenues. In April they are carpeted a rich purple-blue with countless naturalized *Iris germanica* and bordered by fragrant pink *Cyclamen persicum*. Dense patches of the spherical reddish flowers of *Chasmanthe æthiopica* add the finishing touch to this unique sight. When they have finished flowering a tractor cuts the plants right down to neaten the long avenue for the rest of the year. A large variety of Japanese cherries and flowering crab apples, with the white star-shaped blossoms of spiræa, make a beautiful spring background, while the beauty of the showy, rosy-lilac flowers of the Judas tree belies the legend behind the name.

Roses are plentiful in the garden. There is a double border of Meilland's 'Chicago Peace', while the orange grove is underplanted with a bright variety of Meilland's vermilion and red floribunda roses: 'Papa Meilland', 'Suspense', 'Bettina', and 'Pharaoh'. Climbing roses even grow up and into some of the olive trees.

At the end of the olive avenue Mr Norman has made a small arboretum to accommodate favourite trees which might be out of place elsewhere in the garden. Here he has planted five different magnolias, including the massive-leaved *Magnolia delavayi*, a chalk lover, and the delicate and lovely Chinese *M. Wilsonii*. Tree-lovers will appreciate the noble *Cornus nuttallii*, and everyone is struck by the effect of the sun as it turns the robinia into a golden glory amongst the darker trees.

There is also a peony garden at the top of the olive grove for Mr Norman's own pleasure and satisfaction. A wall shelters the fine collection of tree and herbaceous peonies, growing under two alternating Japanese flowering cherries, 'Kanzan' and 'Shimidsu Sakura'. Meilland's climbing rose, 'Danse des Sylphes', shares the wall with honeysuckles, pink *Clematis montana rubra* and a trumpet vine. Above this is a rock garden for dwarf conifers. The avenue leading to a small wisteria-covered Italian temple is lined with a good collection of conifers: two huge thuyas mark the beginning of the avenue, followed by junipers, cedars, chamæcyparis and cryptomerias. Plum and rust-coloured smoke trees, *Cotinus coggygria*, and the brightest honey locust, *Gleditsia triacanthos* 'Sunburst', provide a background of contrasting colours.

A picturesque way to return to the château takes you through the woods overlooking the sea. In December they are carpeted with paper-white narcissi, and in spring they become a glowing mosaic of freesias wherever sunlight pierces through the umbrella pines. Leading off the top of the main olive avenue, the walk is a reminder of all the work and care taken since 1907 to maintain these truly exceptional gardens, carved out of the wild *garrigue*. It is also a walk through time and space, leading from the ancient groves planted by the Romans to the floribunda roses raised in modern France, then back through the original wilderness before emerging in the great formal gardens and the hot massed colours beyond.

La Chèvre d'Or

Biot, near Antibes
(Monsieur et Madame Pierre Champin)

LA CHÈVRE D'OR has a lovely position on a hill facing the old medieval hill-town of Biot. Nearby stand the ruins of an eleventh-century Romanesque tower, built as a mausoleum but believed locally to be the site of a hidden treasure guarded by a mythical golden goat – hence the name of the villa. Pierre and Nicole Champin loved this Mediterranean country-side, its sun and sky, and bought what was then a small *bastide* before the end of the war. In 1944 they began to build a larger house, incorporating the original farmhouse into the new plan – in spite of a dreadful accident when a German landmine exploded, wounding them both severely. The house had no garden, and the only planting they did was to add a few umbrella pines, Mediterranean pines, and a cypress border at the top of the hill. Those first years

RIGHT A double hedge of low clipped box and taller olive trees frame the long rectangular lawn in front of the orangery.
OPPOSITE An Italianate cypress avenue prolongs the central path lined with round clipped orange trees.

A flight of steps leads to the cypress avenue at the top of the hill.

were spent against a simple Virgilian background of olive and orange trees, and the sound of sheep's bells in the early morning.

The first steps towards making a garden were taken in 1951, when an avenue of slender young cypress trees was planted on the rise facing the house. Once the main work on the new house was finished, the ground in front of it was levelled to make a terrace. The old threshing floor at the side of the house was trellised for shade, and retaining walls were added to terrace more of the upper hillside. They found an old stonemason at Antibes, a true artist who knew the art of building the beautiful dry-stone walls that are so much a part of the landscape of the region. He spent years on this slow skilful work. Meanwhile the main terrace, the landings and all the paths were laid with pebbles *en pose de chant* (set on edge), another traditional method seen throughout the south of France in old Provençal village squares. The various designs in contrasting colours are delightful details marking focal points in the garden, and forming the symbol of the house – *la chèvre d'or*

– a goat with a fish·tail. The old olive trees behind the house were enclosed by a walled courtyard and a round space was opened on the sun terrace, around the ancient orange tree. The owners were considered quite mad at the time to have preserved the time-worn orange tree, its trunk so full of holes that it might have been sculpted by Henry Moore – yet it has survived and still bears fruit. Before they bought the property the land was used to grow anemones to sell at the flower market at Nice. An occasional flower still appears in the garden, a rarely uprooted bright trace of the past.

A few old olive trees were added, but most of the trees at La Chèvre d'Or were planted small. It seems impossible that the graceful avenue of cypresses was planted only about thirty years ago. Their slow growth, as with all the trees, has been excellent – a fine lesson in patience for all gardeners. The old pines that bordered the lower road burned like matches in the terrible fire that ravaged the region in 1951. A row of cypresses was planted in their place as extra protection against fire, the nightmare that haunts the minds of all the local inhabitants. Once grown, however, they became a problem, casting too dense and even a shade on the new green garden. Endless discussions with Charles de Noailles, their good friend and neighbour, were resolved when a few died a natural death after a water main burst, thus solving the problem.

Nicole and Pierre Champin's garden was born out of their love and admiration for Italian gardens. The first view of this south-facing garden is caught through the arches of the vaulted entrance to the house. Past the sun terrace a view down the lovely central walk of round clipped orange trees ends at a wall fountain under the elegant avenue of slender cypresses. Echoes of Italy include a number of plant-filled pots standing everywhere on the terrace. Large pots of arum lilies border the edge of the splashing fountain set in a pool between the two flights of steps that lead down from the house to the terrace. Pots of decorative kumquats (kept healthy with regular dressings of dried blood) and lemon trees stand guard beside the wide-arched open-air *salon*. There are pots of white-flowering Portuguese

Diosma ericoides, an interesting plant whose leaves when crushed release a strong, clean, astringent scent, reminiscent of artemisia. Even the fragrant and beautiful *Rhododendron fragrantissimum*, a special present from Charles de Noailles, grows in a giant terracotta pot under the shade of a tree. Smaller pots of special species and scented pelargoniums crowd the steps under the open archways of the house, among them the lemon-scented 'Mabel Grey', the beautiful apple-scented *P. odoratissimum*, in cultivation since 1724, and the busy *P. fragrans variegata* with its heart-shaped leaves. Climbers wreathe the archway of this comfortable *salon* and cover the simple external staircase at the side of the house. A particularly attractive planting combination is the climbing rose 'President Hoover', covered with large well-scented terracotta-flushed deep rose flowers, mixed with the crimson and white flowering *Pandorea jasminoides* and *Jasminum polyanthum*, all growing against the pale apricot wall.

The Champins' garden education was taken in hand by their friend and neighbour Basil Leng, an English expatriate with great taste and extensive knowledge of gardening, who had lived for years in the south of France. He chose most of the plants for the young garden, pruned the shrubs and trees, and all the while advised and taught. He brought many plants from La Mortola, that great abandoned garden at Menton, in order to save them. Often Madame Champin would see a plant she liked and he would set about finding it for her. Rarely was his instinct at fault or a plant variety too invasive. Charles de Noailles would also gladly give assistance when asked. His natural generosity was such that when the Champins had to sack a disastrous gardener who had set the garden back five years, he at once sent them one of his men from the Villa Noailles to keep the garden going.

It was Charles de Noailles who taught them that you must hear the sound of water in a garden, and this is a key element in the long rectangular green garden which stretches from the high cypress-walled lower road to the avenue of orange trees. This deep garden below the sun terrace was a late addition to La

ABOVE The long rectangular green garden is laid out on three levels. OPPOSITE The lovely Japanese wisteria in spring.

Chèvre d'Or. Nicole Champin decided that she wanted to make a 'calm, restful enclosed garden where the pale green box *broderie* would lighten the darker greens of the orange trees and the cypresses'. The box embroideries were first tried in rosemary, which was later abandoned as the extensive watering needed for the grass lawn encouraged the rosemary to become woody. The garden is laid out on three levels, all echoing the lovely contrast of greens. A fountain plays softly into a handsome rectangular stone pool in front of the double line of small rounded trees, set in curving ribbons of box. Two orange trees in ornate terracotta pots add a touch of elegance to the green simplicity. *Magnolia soulangeana* 'Speciosa' and 'Lennei' flower on the second level, underplanted with beds of delightful wild wood violets. A row of orange trees rises out of box-edged squares filled with *Helleborus corsica*, and many-coloured tree peonies, collected jointly by Madame Champin and Charles de Noailles, flourish on the third terrace. Each spring, seeds are carefully gathered from the loveliest of the peonies, particularly the white-flowering varieties, in order to continue the species.

The green garden ends under a series of *planches* (the name given to these terraces in the south of France), all planned and planted in a consciously Japanese spirit. In spring the most beautiful sight in the garden is surely the wisteria pergola in flower. A light bamboo framework covers a small path up the side of the hill, bordered by the high stone retaining wall under the central cypress avenue. Fragrant racemes of Japanese *Wisteria floribunda* 'Macrobotrys' tumble through the open pergola in breathtaking cascades. *Rosa henryi*, originating in eastern China, scrambles through the pergola to flower once the wisteria has finished. Below the pergola a Japanese wisteria makes a small shining tree lit by the full sun, bordered by a group of towering blue-spiked echium. Each year cuttings are taken of the *Echium candicans* to ensure the same excellent intense deep-blue.

The Champins designed a chequerboard garden on the first hillside terrace: squares of cotton lavender alternate with empty squares lined with fine gravel, a design inspired by an abandoned garden they saw during a trip through Japan. A light screening of four *Acacia verticillata*, curiously commonly known as prickly Moses, separates the squares from the higher upper terrace – Pierre Champin's private garden, *le jardin de Monsieur*. Here too the Japanese influence is strongly felt. Pierre Champin has chosen to plant a number of rare trees and shrubs that he had seen and admired for their interesting bark and habit of growth during trips with the International Dendrological Society. Among his treasures are the beautiful small paperbark maple, its old bark curled back to show the cinnamon-coloured underbark, the rare Japanese blue oak, *Quercus glauca*, and the Japanese maple *Acer palmatum*, with its brilliant autumn foliage. Strawberry trees were placed at the top of the sloping terrace: the beautiful cinnamon-red-branched *Arbutus andrachnoides* and the smooth red-brown-barked *Arbutus glandulosa*. A small stream meanders down the middle of the terrace, partly hidden under large plantings of astilbe and Japanese irises. An exuberant *Banksiæ* rose grows up through an olive tree, and the distinctly oriental appearance of the

The lawn leading to the Italianate pavilion.

evergreen *Podocarpus macrophyllus* 'Kusamaki' underlines M. Champin's interest in form.

Over the years the terraces rising above the formal central orange walk have evolved into a series of specialized gardens: a white garden, made by the Champins' daughter, Fleur, then the sundial terrace, the ceanothus terrace and the pink garden. But first of all, long before the green garden, came the equally sophisticated orangery, begun in 1958.

An emerald green lawn with a double hedge of medium-height clipped box and taller clipped olive trees forms a long rectangle in front of an Italianate stone pavilion. The classically simple façade is covered with blue-flowering thunbergia, and the inside walls are trellised for a profusion of climbers: twining dipladenia, blue passion flowers, jasmine, *Solanum jasminoides*, stephanotis, pink-blooming polygonum and *Bignonia purpurea*. *Vitis voinieriana* festoons the ceiling, and huge pots of datura with long creamy-white trumpet flowers outline the wide-arched façade opening on to the immaculate lawn. Pots of orchids, bouvardia, hibiscus and other sub-tropical plants fill every corner of the orangery, the

family's summer dining room and winter garden for fragile plants. A side window gives a glimpse of the small square lotus pond filled with reeds and aquatic plants. A pink *Clematis montana* covers the back of the pavilion, and a collection of trees and shrubs grows just over the double hedge on the higher terrace: *Magnolia grandiflora* and *M. delavayi*, the pink-flowering rounded evergreen raphiolepsis, and the heath-like diplopappus.

The charming lemon pergola walk, just under the orangery, leads to a tiny square house made of sweet bay. A mask by Cartwright, an interesting piece of modern sculpture commissioned by Pierre and Nicole Champin, is faintly visible through the door cut into the laurel. This walk beneath the high wall covered with climbers and under the golden lemons hanging through the green leaves is a delight.

The eighth and uppermost terrace is called *la planche des boules*. Every village in the south of France has a piece of hard flat ground set aside for the local game of *pétanque*, and the centre of this wilder, more southern part of the garden makes an ideal games area.

Here the Champins have planted a collection of sun-lovers: yuccas and palms, such as *Phœnix canariensis* and the long-stalked *P. humilis*, in front of the boundary wall of eucalyptus. A long rectangular pool, a reserve water supply, stands at the far end of the terrace. The ends of the pool are shaded by rough wooden pergolas hung with pale lavender-blue wisteria, and a huge echium with long brilliant blue spikes with red filaments grows in front of the pool. The ground between the backdrop of cypresses and the reservoir is carpeted with bletilla, the magenta-mauve terrestrial orchid, *Iris unguicularis* and pockets of wild cyclamen. Birds singing in two huge parasol pines complete this peaceful Mediterranean composition.

On the way down the flight of steps into the heart of the terrace gardens your eye is caught by endless details: a small bog garden, created accidentally by the overflow from the pool, is planted with a thick bed of large-leaved alocasia; in the pink garden, the autumn-flowering *Hibiscus mutabilis* thrives with *Hibiscus palustris*, the swamp rose-mallow, whose flowers change from pink to red as night falls. In the white garden Fleur, herself a keen and knowledgeable gardener, has planted an exochorda, whose long arching branches are covered in April with large paper-white flowers, and the beautiful xanbocera, a small tree flowering white with a carmine eye. A white lagerstrœmia and a *Viburnum* 'Chenaultii' are also outstanding; and one of the dry-stone walls is covered with *Stauntonia hexaphylla*, a strong evergreen climber with scented mauve flowers in March and April.

A cypress tree marks the entrance to the sundial garden, *le jardin du cadran solaire*. A stone bench stands just off the path in a special bay hedged with *Pittosporum mayi* and box, and a group of rounded rosy-pink *Raphiolepis × delacourii* grows just behind the stone sundial. A superb *Robinia hispida*, the rose acacia, grows near the cypress, behind a jacaranda tree. Other plants include a pink *Lavatera arborea*, *Mimosa* 'Clair de Lune', the creamy-white-flowering *Buddleia auriculata*, the handsome evergreen *Melianthus major*, with tawny-crimson summer flowers, and the dwarf *Lithospermum rosmarinifolium*, covered with bright blue flowers in winter.

Just under Fleur's white garden lies the ceanothus terrace where a large variety of ceanothus provides all shades of blue. Outstanding among varieties are the rich blue 'Delight', the purple-blue *C. rigidissima* and the semi-prostrate *C. divergens*. Silvery *Desmodium perduliaflorum* and the Brazilian *Feijoa selloweana* add to the visual pleasure.

Perhaps the most charming garden at La Chèvre d'Or is the *petite cour*, a small walled courtyard reached through the Champins' bathroom, or through a small door set in the stone wall. Pots of gardenia stand on the edge of a small octagonal fountain whose light jet of water brings a sense of quiet cool to the green shady garden even at the height of summer. This perfumed garden filled with sub-tropical treasures is surrounded by an uneven wall built to enclose the existing olive trees. Pots everywhere, of all sizes, are filled with gardenias, camellias and orchids, including cymbidiums and phalænopsis. A ten-foot-high dark green *Mahonia lomariifolia* grows into the branches of an olive tree, near the strongly scented *Solanum rantonettii* and the lilac-blue summer-flowering *Duranta plumieri*. A huge

Eupatorium atrorubens, cited by Pliny and named after Mithridates Eupator, King of Pontus, who used the plant as an antidote against poison, delights the senses with its sweetly scented Parma blue flowers. This is Nicole Champin's own private place, where 'the calm and repose lets one forget the rest of the world'.

The garden, first planned for the summer months and planted with an abundance of fragrant climbers, datura, tuberoses, desmodium, plumbago, lagerstrœmia and orange trees, progressively became an Easter garden, and finally a garden for all seasons. Madame Champin wrote in the magazine of *Les Amateurs de Jardin* that 'this place made for repose, dreams and forgetfulness, surrounded by its fountains and cypresses, box and orange trees, exists independently and mocks the poor workers we have become, bending over the earth, pruning ... but working and living in the happiness it gives us.'

The semicircular pool below the house adds the sound of water to the main terrace.

Villa Noailles

near Grasse, Alpes-Maritimes
(Le Marquis de Noailles)

THE VILLA NOAILLES is a small eighteenth-century villa set in the high hills above Grasse. The Vicomte Charles de Noailles bought the old house, abandoned and neglected for eighty years, at an auction before the war. The place is small (the Vicomte used to say that he could accommodate no more than six for lunch and a couple of friends to stay overnight), but the garden, visited by guests from all over the world, compensated for this inconvenience. It had two natural advantages: the view down the terraced olive groves and an abundant water supply, even in summer. It seemed an excellent place to plant his favourite camellias and to carry out his idea of adapting plants normally grown in Ireland, such as pieris and drimys. But it was only after the war that he left his previous house and garden on the coast at Hyères to come and settle here and begin the work which turned the garden into a masterpiece.

Water is life in a garden: its essential usefulness, its sound and its beauty ... The most important thing in my garden is the spring from the mountain, which made me decide to settle in Grasse having suffered for years from the rationing of water at Hyères. Right at the top of the property there is a small tunnel in which a man could just stand upright; it penetrates about sixty-five yards into the hill and provides the water supply for the fountains, cascades, streams and water-basins. Some gardens are said to be perfumed ... I would say this one sings.

The sound of water welcomes you to the Villa Noailles, as you walk down a few steps into the courtyard beyond the faded blue nail-studded door set in the outer wall. The sound

The hedges at the Villa Noailles are treated architecturally.

comes from a fountain set in the wall, just
above some terracotta pots filled with glossy
camellias. Further on, another wall fountain,
once a washing trough, makes a ravishing
picture as water slowly trickles down from the
water shelves and over the wall clothed in
green *Helxine soleirolii* and *Adiantum venustrum*.
Ornamental fleurs-de-lis and obelisks are
carved in calcareous tufa, and altogether the
fountain is a small rustic evocation of the
terrace of a hundred fountains at the Villa
d'Este. The wall is sheltered under a bower
roofed with *Banksiæ* roses which cast a gold and
green shade. A pergola planted with alternating Judas trees covers the first part of the upper
walk: four rosy-purple-flowering *Cercis sil-
quastrum* to one white, a scheme suggested
by Russell Page. Further along the path the
upper bank is carpeted with a collection of
cyclamens from Corsica, Crete, Persia and
mainland Greece, shaded by a loose box hedge
and sweet bay, *Laurus nobilis*. A beautiful and
highly fragrant rhododendron, *R. fragrantissimum*, grows by the orchid-pink-flowering
camellia 'Donation'.

The upper woodland walk ends at a stone

fountain set in a hedge in front of a misty view
of distant hills. Another walk traces the descending terraces down to the bottom of the garden,
each turn bringing new delights, for the
garden is filled with small pavilions, pools
and fountains. Seats give views of the garden
from all angles in both light and shade. First
comes the enclosed octagonal herb and iris
garden, with its simple wooden gate set in a
myrtle hedge under a slender white double arch
wreathed in *Clematis cirrhosa*. A round-domed
garden house, a *turquerie* made of sweet bay,
stands behind a central hexagonal basin filled
with water-lilies. Lower down the walk a
bamboo pergola hung with wisteria lightly
shades a collection of camellias, amongst them
Camellia 'Directeur Lontil', *C.* 'Bahaud Litou'
and 'Moreiro da Silva'. All the plants and
shrubs throughout the garden are clearly and
elegantly labelled. A special magnolia is
planted here, a present from Mr Hillier:
Magnolia Campbellii mollycomata, the Himalayan
pink tulip tree with large waxy flowers like
magenta water-lilies. Rare plants are set in
small rectangular beds, including winter-
flowering *Iris stylosa*, the white-flowering bul-

bous pancratium, *Agapanthus* 'Lambet' and the mauve ophiopogon. *Amaryllis belladonna* grow around the rectangular pool at the end of the garden.

Lower down the hill a group of rare shrubs in shades of blue illustrates M. de Noailles' talent as both gardener and designer. Sycopsis is grown as a small tree near dramatic blue-spiked echiums, regrettably too delicate to survive further north, and an imposing blue-black-fruited *Mahonia lomariifolia*. The holly-like *Osmanthus illicifolius*, a thick *Carylopsis pauciflora*, grey-leaved *Olearia scilloniensis*, pale blue-flowering hebe and modest forget-me-nots and scillas complete this composition of blue, grey and dark green.

Another rare and striking plant bordering the path is the thirty-year-old yucca-like *Beschorneria yuccoides*. The six-foot-long red stems, hung with bright green flowers with red bracts, tower behind a raised circular water-lily pool banked with *Pittosporum mayi*, Jerusalem sage, abelia and massed agapanthus.

Hundred-year-old olive trees grow on the terraces stretching along the hillside. Years ago, Charles de Noailles acquired a flock of white sheep to graze under the olives, which had been lavishly underplanted with thousands of narcissi, grouped in different varieties. The lovely effect attracted the sheep, which wrought such destruction that they were rapidly given away.

Another failure of this kind took place some fifteen years ago, when the Vicomte read an advertisement in *Country Life* to the effect that some budgerigars that had been trained at Woburn Abbey to live at liberty during the day and return to their aviary at nightfall, were being sold by the late Duke of Bedford's estate. The idea of the tiny green, blue and yellow birds flashing jewel-like in the silver-grey trees was delightful, and they were duly imported after great difficulties. Once established, however, their ducal education was forgotten, and they nested in the olive trees, prey to all the local cats. The survivors now live in the charming *volière* at the bottom of the path, the green walls set with two Portuguese blue-tile pictures. The charming effect of a house covered in tiny thread-like plants was easily achieved by using a chicken-wire framework

TOP The play of a fountain above the central flight of stone stairs.

ABOVE A tiled pavilion between the kitchen garden and the budgerigar aviary.

on the walls as a support for muehlenbeckia. The same idea was used at La Chèvre d'Or at Biot (pp 194–201), where muehlenbeckia grows underneath the stone steps in the en-

LEFT The water shelves, a rustic fantasy inspired by the terraces of one hundred fountains at the Villa d'Este, are roofed with Banksian roses.
ABOVE Stonework gives structure to the garden.
OPPOSITE 'Water is life in a garden'. Charles de Noailles.

RIGHT This marble face is set in the wall of a muehlenbeckia covered tool-house.
BELOW The entrance courtyard is filled with terracotta pots of camellias, in the Italian fashion.
OPPOSITE ABOVE Sunlight through the branches of the laburnum in the kitchen garden.
OPPOSITE BELOW A flight of stone steps borders the channel of a small stream in the middle of the garden.

trance patio. Near the aviary there is a long pool loosely edged in box and beyond is another camellia garden. *Camellia* 'August Desfosse' was planted twenty-five years ago and blooms next to the red and white variegated flowers of *C.* 'Kelvingtoniana' and the salmon pink 'Drama Girl'.

Nearby is the kitchen garden pavilion. An arched passage leads into the old vegetable garden, hedged with *Euonymus microphyllus*. The garden is bare now, for the Vicomte decided that a *potager* was a pleasant but unreasonable luxury and had only begun to redesign the area before his death. He had already surrounded the old wisterias, grown as standards, with a design of box globes set in open crosses of *Bergenia crassifolia*. Typically, this exceptional gardener continued to plan for the future, although handicapped by arthritis and great age. Chairs were placed throughout the garden so that he could sit, rest and enjoy it at leisure. He continued to make notes, but left none for the *potager*, as he had not yet found a satisfactory solution. The ground remains bare under the wisterias.

A rounded rock garden was made below the aviary and kitchen garden pavilion. An amusing *trop-plein*, or overflow fountain, made with two balanced pieces of bamboo, stands near a planting of white bearded irises and blue alliums. Water falls from one bamboo pipe into the hollow lip of the other until, the balance lost, it tips down, spilling water into a pool – an ancient irrigation technique.

An alluvial meadow lies at the bottom of the six terraces, bordered by a stream which almost dries up in summer in spite of the water from the fountains and pools throughout the garden. The meadow is planted with Japanese flowering cherries and magnolias, M. de Noailles' favourite trees. In 1976 he wrote a small article on the magnolias at Grasse for the International Dendrological Year Book, which is worth quoting from to explain his love for these beautiful trees. 'For as long as I can remember, I have been attracted by thick waxy flowers. To this day I have never taken much interest in papery plants, cistus, abutilon, and so forth.' He goes on to explain that two of the magnolias, the *Magnolia soulangeana* and *M. kobus*, were transplanted from Hyères to

Grasse, and he gives their order of flowering at the Villa: '*Magnolia denudata*, *M. kobus*, *M. soulangiana* in its diverse varieties – "Alexandrina", "Alba", "Lennei" ... the last to flower. *Magnolia virginiana*, planted twenty-five years ago (now thirty-two) by the pool has grown well but never flowered.' It did eventually bloom, and M. de Noailles was able to enjoy its marvellous scent. The magnolias were carefully placed. Some, like the *grandiflora* and *delavayi*, were to be used as windbreaks; all were planted to take best advantage of their shape, size and time of flowering.

The cherries, complained M. de Noailles, were worn out, having reached and passed their maturity, but they were also impossible to replace owing to the shade cast by the magnolias. In spite of his depreciation of them, there is no more unforgettable sight in the garden than the Yoshino cherry, *Prunus yedoensis* 'Shidare Yoshino', its arched and weeping branches supported by bamboo poles when it forms an almond-scented blush-white pavilion in the spring. A *Paulownia tomentosa* is a superb sight, flowering deep blue in late April, and another interesting tree is the *Davidia vilmoriniana*, the handkerchief tree, so called because of the large white bracts fancifully likened to pocket handkerchiefs. But the tree which was M. de Noailles' greatest pride is the *Metasequoia glyptostroboides*, a present from his Belgian friends and fellow dendrologists, the de Belders. Planted in 1952, it was already over seventy feet high after twenty-nine years. Metasequoia owners from all over the world take measure of this particular tree and regular communications are made; M. de Noailles was always proud to say that his metasequoia had the fastest rate of growth in France. The dawn redwood, an extremely hardy tree easily grown from seed, is also a tree of great beauty, with feathery foliage, a bright young green in summer, turning tawny pink and old gold in autumn.

The lowest terrace, next to the magnolia meadow, is planted with the choicest camellias and other rare shrubs imported largely from Hilliers in England, including the snowdrop tree, *Halesia carolina*, its branches covered with white nodding bell-shaped flowers and the magnolia-like evergreen *Michelia fuscata*, with

small glossy leaves and purple-brown, insignificant flowers, curiously scented like pear-drops. The bright red young growth of *Pieris formosa forestii* 'Forest Flame' makes a brilliant display near the elegant *Cornus kousa*, with strawberry-like fruits. A muehlenbeckia-covered tool house stands at the end of the terrace, near the central garden steps. Water spills from the smiling lips of a white marble face set in the plant-covered wall, to fall into a shell basin.

A long flight of stone steps bordered by a small stream leads up the middle of the garden, from a stone pyramid to just under the Aldobrandini column. The steps are divided in the middle to make a passage for pushing wheelbarrows – a glimpse of Charles de Noailles' endless thoughtful concern over even the slightest detail. The pyramid, bought from an antique dealer in Mougins as Roman, was later discovered to be the stolen tomb of a Napoleonic general. Underneath it grows a huge aloe-like *Yucca parviflora engelmannii* with giant blood-red spikes and drooping tomato-red golden-throated flowers. There is a mixed planting of shrubs behind the tomb: the silver variegated-leaved *Cornus controversa variegata*, a rare orange-flowering *Osmanthus fragrans* 'Auriantiacus' and bronze-red *Ribes odoratum* × *sanguineum*.

High on the corner of the *Banksia*-covered retaining wall, up the steps and past the pyramid, the slender jet of a fountain falls into a high fluted basin, an uneven curtain of falling water splashing in harmony with the gently rushing stream beside the steps. But the most spectacular fountain is the Aldobrandini column at the bottom of the steps, a half-sized replica of one seen and admired at the Villa Aldobrandini at Frascati. Water spills forth irregularly and unexpectedly from the top of the Roman column and spirals down into a little pool. A trained conifer, *Cedrus atlantica* 'Pendula', underplanted with oxalis stands behind it, together with the long rounded yew hedges which enclose the peony garden. There are no more than two plants of each variety.

When Charles de Noailles moved to the villa, he found two-hundred-year-old box hedges which had become impenetrable and quite ungovernable. He cut them back ruthlessly, and for two years they looked quite dead; then as new growth appeared he pruned them each year to improve their shape. The yew hedges lining the two upper gardens are now very rounded and cut low at one end. Other hedges throughout the garden are made from a large variety of plants to avoid repetition.

Two Chinese-style pavilions with tiled roofs mark the outer corners of the upper terraces: one is used as a wine-cellar, and the other is a charming summer house overlooking the garden. A triangular 'room' made of box houses a fountain cushioned in *Helxine soleirolii*, and behind the hedged wall overlooking the upper gardens and under the façade of the villa, is an eighteenth-century circular water garden. The balcony shelters a tiled outdoor *salon* designed by Emilio Terry. The walls of the villa are covered with scented *Holbœllia latifolia* and purple-flowering *Akebia quinata* and the box-hedged beds are filled with *Scilla peruviana*. In 1969 Charles de Noailles added pink and white Japanese carp, brought from the Japanese Embassy in Paris, to the pool. Unlike the sheep and the budgerigars from Woburn these caused no major problems, apart from their refusal to eat European food. Their habitual nourishment was imported from Japan and so they grew from year to year.

The Vicomte Charles de Noailles died in April 1981. A few months after his death I spent a long afternoon at the Villa Noailles with his old gardener, Pierre Cespuglio. Slowly we traced Charles de Noailles' usual walk through the garden: along the top walk under the Judas pergola, down the side path to the magnolia meadow and up the stone steps to the house. We stopped to admire the mastery of each design and composition. Pierre drew my attention to every plant that had delighted the Vicomte, telling me where it had been found and when planted. Each halt recalled the long past they had shared in the garden.

On such summer afternoons the water of the fountains and basins, streams and pools – each designed and positioned with care by Charles de Noailles, whose greatest joy was the harmony of their sounds – still fill the garden of the Villa Noailles with their endless splashing and murmuring.

OPPOSITE 'What golden hour of life, what glittering moment will ever equal the pain its loss can cause?' Paul Valéry, *Mauvaises Pensées et Autres*.

Picture Acknowledgments

The authors and publisher would like to thank the following photographers, institutions and agencies by whose kind permission the illustrations are reproduced:

François Pereire pages 58, 59, 61, 62 and 63
Roger-Viollet page 69 (below) and page 116 (above)
Musée Marmottan page 118 (above) *photo Routhier*
Agence Top pages 128, 129, 130 and 131 *photos P. Hinous*

All other photographs are by Robert César.

Bibliography

Recommended Reading

W.H. Adams, *The French Garden 1500–1800*, George Braziller, New York, 1979

E.A. Bowles, *My Garden in Spring*, David & Charles Reprints, London, 1972

E.A. Bowles, *My Garden in Summer*, David & Charles Reprints, London, 1972

E.A. Bowles, *My Garden in Autumn & Winter*, David & Charles Reprints, London, 1972

Beth Chatto, *The Dry Garden*, Dent, London, 1978

F.R. Cowell, *The Garden as a Fine Art*, Weidenfeld & Nicolson, London, 1979.

M. Duval, *The King's Garden*, University Press of Virginia, Charlottesville, 1982

Jardins en France, 1760–1820, Caisse Nationale des Monuments Historiques et des Sites, Paris

Gertrude Jekyll (most of her books are now being reprinted by the Antique Collectors' Club – all are well worth reading):

Gertrude Jekyll, *Colour Schemes for the Flower Garden*, Country Life Library, London, 1914

Gertrude Jekyll, *Wall and Water Gardens*, Country Life Library, London, 1920

Gertrude Jekyll & E. Mawley, *Roses for English Gardens*, Country Life Library, London, 1902

Robin Lane Fox, *Variations on a Garden*, Macmillan, London, 1974

Robin Lane Fox, *Better Gardening*, London, 1982

Christopher Lloyd, *The Well Tempered Garden*, Collins, London, 1970

Christopher Lloyd, *Foliage Plants*, Collins, London, 1973

Christopher Lloyd, *Clematis*, Collins, London, 1977

Russell Page, *The Education of a Gardener*, Collins, London, 1962 (now in reprint)

G. Rémon, *Les Jardins*, Flammarion, Paris, 1943

Royal Horticultural Society, *Some Good Garden Plants*, London, 1964

C. Thacker, *Histoire des Jardins*, Denoël, 1981

Mrs Desmond Underwood, *Grey and Silver Plants*, Collins, London, 1971

General Reference Books

W.J. Bean, *Trees & Shrubs Hardy in the British Isles* (eighth edition), 4 vols, John Murray, London, 1970

Peter Coats, *Great Gardens of Britain*, Weidenfeld & Nicolson, London, 1967

Peter Coats, *Great Gardens of Europe*, Weidenfeld & Nicolson, London, 1977

Hillier, *Hillier's Manual of Trees & Shrubs*, David & Charles, 1972

B. Mathew, *Dwarf Bulbs*, Batsford, London, 1969

S. Millar Gault, *The Dictionary of Shrubs*, Ebury Press & Michael Joseph, 1975

S. Millar Gault & Patrick M. Synge, *The Dictionary of Roses*, 1971

I. Pizzetti & H. Cocker, *Flowers – A Guide for Your Garden*, 2 vols, Harry N. Abrams, 1975.

H. Randall, *Irises*, Batsford, London, 1969

Reader's Digest, *Encylopaedia of Garden Plants and Flowers*, Reader's Digest Association, 1971

Royal Horticultural Society, *Dictionary of Gardening*, 4 vols + Supplement, Oxford University Press, 1956

Graham Stuart Thomas, *Shrub Roses of Today*, Phoenix House, 1962

Graham Stuart Thomas, *The Old Shrub Roses*, Phoenix House, 1955

Graham Stuart Thomas, *Climbing Roses Old & New*, Phoenix House, 1965

Graham Stuart Thomas, *Colour in the Winter Garden*, Dent & Sons, 1957

Graham Stuart Thomas, *Perennial Garden Plants*, Dent & Sons, 1976

Graham Stuart Thomas, *Plants for Ground Cover*, Dent & Sons, 1976

Patrick M. Synge, *Collins Guide to Bulbs*, Collins, 1961

Patrick M. Synge & Roy Hay, *The Dictionary of Garden Plants in Colour*, Michael Joseph, London, 1969

Books and Catalogues on Claude Monet

Gustave Geffroy, *Claude Monet, sa vie, son temps, son œuvre*, Paris, 1922

C. Joyes, *Monet at Giverny*, Mathews Miller Dunbar, London, 1975

Gerald van der Kemp, *A Visit to Giverny*, Editions d'Art Lys, Versailles, 1980

Daniel Wildenstein, *Claude Monet*, vol III, La Bibliothèque des Arts, Lausanne, Paris, 1979

Catalogues:

Hommage à Claude Monet, Ministère de la Culture et de la Communication, Paris, 1980

Monet's Years at Giverny, Metropolitan Museum of Art, New York, 1978

Index